Changing Tides

Changing Tides

World War II Occupation and Independence in the Philippines

Isabel Yumol Jennings

State House Press
Buffalo Gap, Texas

Library of Congress Cataloging-in-Publication Data

Jennings, Isabel Yumol
Changing Tides: World War II Occupation and Independence in the Philippines
p. cm.
Includes Bibliographical references and index.
ISBN 978-1-933337-68-5 (pbk. alk. paper)
ISBN- 1-933337-68-0 (pbk. alk. paper)
1. Philippines World War II 2. Occupation Philippines World War II-Biography
3. Women in Philippines World War II 4. World War II

This paper meets the requirements of ANSI/NISO, Z39.48-1992 (permanence of paper)

Binding materials have been chosen for durability
I. Title.

"Cataloging-in-Publication Data available from the Library of Congress"

Manufactured in the United States

First Printing

State House Press
P.O. Box 818
Buffalo Gap, Texas 79508
325-572-3974 · 325-572-3991 (fax)
www.tfhcc.com

Printed in the United States of America
Distributed by Texas A&M University Press Consortium
800-826-8911
www.tamupress.com

ISBN-13: 978-1-933337-68-5
ISBN-10: 1933337-68-0
Book Design by Rosenbohm Graphic Design

Dedicated to my brothers Rey, Benching, and Benny

Contents

Foreword

Isabel (Lita) Yumol Jennings has an important story to tell. It is a story that sadly too many Americans are unaware of. It is a story of how two friendly and resilient people—the Filipinos and their American allies—overcame almost impossible odds to defeat the Japanese invasion and occupation during World War II. Lita tells her personal story, first seen both through the eyes of a young Filipino girl born in Manila and then later refocused through the lens of an older, much wiser woman—a woman who has accomplished much, not only surviving the war imposed on her nation, but also someone who, during her lifetime, went on to garner numerous awards and accolades. In *Changing Tides*, Lita covers the complexities of war by telling a personal story—a story of how her family's love, courage, and perseverance enabled them to endure the darkest of times following the Japanese invasion in 1941.

I refer to Isabel Yumol Jennings simply as *Lita*. Lita is her social name, lovingly given by her family, shortened from Isabel. Isabel is her professional name. Maybe I should refer to her as Doctor Jennings because she went on to earn a Ph.D. in Applied Linguistics at the University of Texas. As with so many Americans, opportunity ultimately beckoned Lita to the United States, where she later chose to become a U.S. citizen. Her husband, Frank, was an extremely knowledgeable historian and worked for the Air Force as a high-ranking civilian in the Pentagon's Public Affairs office; he was also a noted author. He coined the term *aerospace* when the Department of Defense was trying to come up with a term to describe the region including the earth's atmosphere and outer space.

Frank mentored most of the Air Force public affairs officers, including me. I along, with many other U.S. Air Force officers, owe Frank much for our professional growth and success. Lita was always by his side at the many social events my wife Jeannie and I attended. I really don't know Isabel that well, but I sure know Lita. She is a gracious, witty, intelligent, attractive woman, so quick to smile—a person who has blessed me and many others with her many years of friendship. Lita's story proves her to be more than the intellectual equal of Frank. Although he is now looking at us from above, I know that he would agree.

Those of us who were born in the United States have never known conquest by a foreign government. Occupied yes, but conquest no. American Indians were not so lucky. The early Americans settled the colonies and then fought the British for their independence. The British were not the big losers in this fight; Americans Indians were. Their lands were taken, treaties broken, and their lifestyles and cultures almost destroyed.

During World War II, many European nations were also invaded, conquered, and almost destroyed by the Germans and their allies. Because of the stories told in our history books, most Americans know something about the great world war that raged in both Europe and the Pacific. During World War II, both Germany and Japan ravished nations and peoples on an unprecedented scale. For a while, it was touch and go who would win. Fortunately, the United States and its allies went on to defeat Germany and Japan.

As with the European front, the Pacific front during World War II was a ferocious fight. One nation that was horrifically brutalized in the Pacific theatre by the Japanese was the Philippines. The bombing of Pearl Harbor on December 8, 1941, was a prelude of things to come for the Filipino people—inhabitants of the more than the seven thousand islands of the Philippines. As Lita explains, when Pearl Harbor was attacked, Philippine President Manuel Quezon and General Douglas MacArthur took to the airwaves. They told the Filipino people to make emergency preparations because the Japanese were soon going to attack. It came all too soon. Only ten hours after the attack on Pearl Harbor, Japan attacked the Philippines.

Lita writes that as people were intently listening to their radios, they heard the disturbing news that the American bases in Angeles, Pampanga, and the Iba airfield in Zambales and the Subic naval base in Olongapo were bombed and destroyed. Next to be attacked and destroyed was the Sangley Point Naval Base, south of Manila. General MacArthur then told the people of Manila to evacuate to the provinces because the Japanese would be bombing the city in advance of an invasion.

Lita's book is not an encyclopedic explanation of the battle accounts of the war inflicted on her nation. Rather, it is her personal story of how she and her family pulled together, and through love and courage and sacrifice, survived those perilous times.

However, it is worth noting some of the historical context that frames Lita's book. The United States and her allies quickly marshaled the armed forces of the Philippines and augmented them with allied personnel and equipment. However, during the first half of 1942, the Japanese had overrun most of the nation. Guerrilla resistance against the Japanese continued from the beginning and throughout the war. Uncaptured Filipino army units, a communist insurgency and supporting American agents all played a role in the resistance.

The Liberation of the Philippines finally began in earnest with an American amphibious landing on the eastern Philippine island of Leyte on October 20, 1944. This was to mark the beginning of the end. However, hostilities continued until August 1945.

Estimates of how many vary, but many thousands of Filipino people and their allies died during World War II. They fought hard to win back the freedom for this island people. Most know how all this ends. The United States, the Philippines, and their allies went on to defeat the Japanese. However, the victory took a great toll in national treasure and lives. Fortunately, the allies were victorious, and the Philippines went on to become their own nation.

Lita ends her story with a poignant account of the ceremony at the national park of the United States awarding independence to the Philippines. Reading that account shot chills up my spine and the tears were close behind.

Thank you Lita for writing this marvelous book. Your personal story of your family's love, courage, and perseverance will not only entertain, but it will also inform. Your book will also inspire those reading it to see that freedom and justice are values and beliefs held by all peoples—and are worth fighting for, and if need be, even dying for.

Gene Townsend, Colonel, USAF (Ret.)*

* Colonel Townsend served twenty-eight years in the U.S. Air Force. He served as Editor of *Airman Magazine*, Official Magazine of the Air Force, and as Editor and Publisher of *The European Stars and Stripes.*

Preface

History looks at events from the outside. It records dates, places, countries and their leaders, the power struggle, motives and outcomes, treaties, and so on. A memoir looks at the same events from the inside, from the perspective of the people who have nothing to do with the events but who find themselves in the crossfire and often become collateral damage. It tells of how they survive the battles, how they cope under a repressive regime and carry on with their lives with as much semblance of normalcy as possible—celebrating their personal joys and triumphs so as to push aside the pervasive national sadness, deeply mourning and grieving for their personal losses and tragedies that diminish the tragedy of being a subjugated people—and how they hope and pray for the liberation that will end the constant fear for one's life, the pain and suffering, the deprivation. . . . This is my story.

For those who have never experienced an invasion and conquest of their country, my memoir opens a window of information beyond speculation. For those who know little about the role of the Philippines during World War II, this is a story that needs to be told.

Acknowledgments

The writing of any piece, be it in Arts and Letters, in Humanities, or in Science depends on a lot of people who show interest, ask questions, and provide feedback, comments, and encouragement. And such is the case in writing my memoir about World War II in the Philippines. A chance narration of certain events to my Spanish Conversation Group (*Las Chicas Picaras*) piqued interest and questions from Marlene Merritt, Joyce Popelar, Charlotte Randolph, and Maxine Zimmerman; they were enthusiastic about the sample pages I had already written. When I mentioned the project to Bob Hunter, my late husband Frank's colleague in the Air Force Public Affairs field, he asked to see a sample. He pointed out certain informational gaps of which I wasn't aware because of how close I was to the events. He kept encouraging me to finish the story because, as he put it, "we are not aware that these things were going on in the Philippines." The same sentiment came from Dr. Bruce Winders, Curator at the Alamo, who, after reading some chapters, said, "this story needs to be told." The Yoes—Deck (who served in the U.S. Navy) and Mary (a retired nurse) —good friends at the exercise and fitness center, served as reader and critic and made me re-examine facts and some events I had set aside. And last, but not least, Gene Townsend, who kindly accepted my invitation to write the Foreword to this book, looked at the sample chapters with the trained eyes of a professional editor and writer, and saw and appreciated the human interest in the historical event and its informative potential.

Special thanks go to Donald S. Frazier, President and CEO, and to Scott Clowdus, Chief Operating Officer, both at the McWhiney History Education Group that houses State House Press, for their commitment to publishing my story; and to Claudia Gravier Frigo, Project Manager, for overseeing the production of this book.

To all these friends I owe a deep gratitude Without their input and encouragement, I would not have been inspired, nor have found the confidence, to finish writing my story.

Isabel Yumol Jennings

October 2015

Japanese Invasion: December 8, 1941–March 1942

Life-Changing News

On the bright, sunny, and pleasantly warm morning of December 8, 1941, as we walk home after Mass celebrating the Feast of the Immaculate Conception at the Church of the University of Santo Tomas, three blocks from our street, Mr. Villa, one of Father's chess mates and the neighborhood electrician, rushes toward us and tells Father,

> Tom, according to my short-wave radio last night, the U.S. Military installation at Pearl Harbor in Hawaii was bombed and destroyed in a sneak attack by the Japanese who are now on their way here to the Philippines to attack us. On regular radio this morning, Gen. Douglas MacArthur and President Manuel Quezon announced it and asked the people to make all kinds of emergency preparations.

I am nine and in the fifth grade at the Sta. Isabel College, a convent school for girls run by the nuns of the Daughters of Charity of St. Vincent de Paul from Spain, located across the Pasig River in Intramuros. My brother, Tommy, is three and we now have a baby brother, Rey, born May 12.

Father turns to Mother and says, "Go on home and gather up large supplies of water and non-perishable food, as well as candles, matches, flashlights, batteries, and blankets, and medical supplies. Get plenty of firewood for cooking and cook up the perishable food."

Then he turns to me and says, "Lita, run to all the houses on our street and spread the news and alert the people on storing up supplies."

Most people do not listen to the radio early in the morning; they wait till 10:00 or 11:00 for the talk shows, melodramas, or comedies. Tommy wants to come with me but I tell him to help Mother or watch over Rey because Mother will be busy.

Father and Mr. Villa go back to his house to listen for more news and call the other household heads for a meeting on how to secure our neighborhood. When I get home, Tommy is playing with Rey, Mother and the maid are busy filling up all available pots, bottles, pitchers, and other containers with water. *Ate* Nene, Mother's youngest sister, who is three years older than me and who has been with us since their mother died, is packing pillowcases with all kinds of supplies. On one corner is a big box full of cans of Milkmaid condensed milk and another containing cartons of Klim powder milk for Rey's food.

When Mother sees me she says, "call *Tatay* Iboy (Mother's father) and ask if they have heard the news."

I go to the telephone, the black rectangular box set high up against the wall so I have to get on a chair to reach it. I lift the earphone, a small trumpet-like object that hangs between two prongs that come out of the side of the box and attached to the box by an electric wire, and place the wide end to my ear, dial the number on the round dial at the front of the box and speak to a smaller trumpet just above the dial. *Tatay* Iboy wants to talk to Mother so I hand her the earphone.

Father comes home late that night; I am still up and I ask him why the Japanese will attack us. He says, "The Philippines is a Commonwealth of the United States and we're friends, and so the Japanese think of us as enemies."

Classes are canceled. Everybody is glued to the radio and we hear that the U.S. air base in Angeles, Pampanga, and the Iba airfield in Zambales, as well as the Subic naval base in Olongapo, all North of Manila, have been bombed and destroyed. Then, the Sangley Point Naval Base in Cavite, South of Manila, is also destroyed. Philippine President Manuel Quezon tells the people to be calm, to prepare well for emergencies. And "blackout" (no visible lights from houses and streets at night) is ordered throughout the city. To comply, thick, black drapes are hung on windows at night, street lights are turned off, and curfew is imposed.

After several days, General MacArthur urges the people of Manila to evacuate to the provinces because the Japanese will be bombing the city preparatory to an invasion. My parents let the maid go when she says she wants to be with her family in the province.

Tatay Iboy and Tiyeng, Mother's oldest sister, who is not married, arrive and say that we should all go to Mabatang, a small village in Abucay, Bataan, hometown of *Nanay* Toria (Mother's mother). They practically own this small town; every villager is some sort of a relative. They own most of the rice fields, the only rice granary (a rectangular warehouse for storing sacks of rice) in town, several fishponds, and many home poultry and piggeries. We would never go hungry. Moreover, there will be lots of relatives and maids to help Mother.

Father informs Mr. Villa and their other chess mates of our plan and he wishes them good luck and safety in their own plans. Mr. Villa says, "We're staying, Tom. We do not have a province with relatives to go to."

Some of the others say the same thing. "We all hope the Japanese would choose particular targets of military importance to hit and not just everything, including residential areas, just to destroy the city."

We bring everything that Mother has packed—supplies and clothing—pile into *Tatay* Iboy's Packard driven by Berto, the chauffeur, and drive north out of Manila. It is a happy trip. Tommy is enjoying everything—the scenery, the ride. It is his first automobile ride.

When we arrive in Mabatang, *Tata* (granduncle) Julian, the widower of *Nana* (grandaunt) Chayong, grandmother's youngest sister, meets us and accompanies us to the family house of *Tatay* Iboy and *Nanay* Toria. *Lolo* (grandfather), Anong (*Nanay* Toria's youngest brother), and his wife and five children arrive in their Cadillac. They are assigned to stay in one of the larger homes of their cousins.

Life is wonderful; lots of different food to eat, many grandaunts who love to cook snacks for the children, plenty of cousins to play with outside the houses, in the yards, on the streets, in the rice fields, and by the seashore close to the fishponds. Three-year-old Tommy is having the time of his life, chasing chickens, climbing the low reclining trunk of the mango tree, playing in the clear spring-fed creek, and bathing at the huge pump of the artesian well in the center of town. When it rains, all the children play and splash and bathe in the rain, later to be picked up, dried, and dressed by the maids. And I do the same things because I am Tommy's guardian, having taken care of him from infancy because Mother, who was sickly and weak from attacks of rheumatism, could not carry him around or play with him. But, he likes it best when I read to him or play jigsaw puzzles or bring out the coloring books on some of those stormy days in December.

Tommy shows an unselfish side, even as a child. Because I am the first child, and the oldest in my family, everyone gives me the first choice and the best, as is expected in a hierarchical cultural system. This hierarchical system is preserved further by using honorific titles preceding first names. So I am *ate* [ah-teh] Lita not only to Tommy but to all the children younger than I, as *Ate* Nene, mother's youngest sister, is *ate* to me because she is older. And Tommy, as the older brother, is *kuya* [koo-yah] Tommy to Rey. Moreover, as the child of Tom Yumol, greatly admired and highly respected person and lawyer, and of Tacing, idolized daughter of the family, I am catered to and pampered. Tommy just stands by when I get all the attention and goodies. He never grabs nor complains. I, however, wait till he receives his portion, then I share some of mine with him, especially food. Father says that very young children should never feel deprived because they do not understand it.

We celebrate Christmas Eve with a midnight Mass and snacks afterward. As usual, Christmas Day is celebrated with lots of food and gifts and festivities. Then news arrives that General MacArthur and his U.S. troops are retreating to Bataan and Corregidor where they will make a last stand. *Lolo* Anong decides to take his family back to Manila because he is worried about his business and their home.

As the last of the U.S. troops and Philippine Scouts, who are part of the U.S. armed forces, leave Manila, they blow up Calumpit Bridge, a major road out of and into Manila. Our hopes of returning home to Manila die. The Japanese enter Manila unopposed after some bombardment of the city, although General MacArthur has declared it an "Open City" to preserve many of the historic and grand buildings.

When it appears that Bataan is going to be a battlefield, many people decide to leave the cities and towns and hide out in the mountains and forests. *Tata* Julian and his young sons, *Nana* Guida and her family, and others decide to stay. They say,

> This is our home—we were born and grew up here; we built up this town. We would never abandon it; we need to keep it going. And if we would die here, so be it. But you [looking at all of us] need to seek safety in the forests. And when things have settled and it is safe, then you can come out and return.

So we start storing and packing again. The Packard was commandeered earlier by some retreating soldiers, as well as the horses and carts and *carabaos* (water buffalo work animals). Berto has joined the soldiers. We have to walk and carry what we have packed. Father, *Tatay* Iboy, and Tiyeng carry the bigger and heavier loads; Mother carries Rey in a diaper sling tied around her neck. I carry a small cloth bag with one change of clothing each for me and Tommy and two towels, slung over one shoulder.

A Trek through Unfamiliar Terrain

We start out early this morning. We walk five kilometers, sometimes seven, across or sometimes along rice fields; stop now and then to rest or to eat. Not a word of complaint or whimper from three-year-old Tommy. But often Father or *Tatay* Iboy would pick him up and carry him when they notice that he is looking very tired and slowing down. We sleep out in the open under the trees at one end of the rice field. Fortunately, Tiyeng has brought a wide mat made of interwoven palm leaves, which is spread over some dried rice straws gathered from haystacks, pillows, blankets, and a big mosquito net which is hung over us by tying the top four corners to nearby trees. Tiyeng sleeps at one end of the mat, then *Ate* Nene, seven-month-old Rey, Mother, Father, me, Tommy, and *Tatay* Iboy.

This first night I can not sleep; it is dark, and I am cold, and frightened of the *tiktik* (black bird that announces the presence of a vampire according to folklore) and the *capre* (folkloric ogres on top of trees who pounce and snatch sleeping children). Tommy must have sensed it, he snuggles closer to me and holds my hand; I finally fall asleep tired out from the long walk.

We are several families who leave together. Now my family is the only one left behind. We have to go slowly and stop often because of Mother who is not strong and is one-month pregnant. Because we are never too far from a stream that we are following, we sponge-bathe daily and soak our feet. Tiyeng boils and stores spring water for drinking. After several days, we are met by some of the men of the other families. We cross the stream, go through a thicket, and come out to a clearing. There are several huts and one is assigned to us. Downstairs is a big room that has the living room and dining area; behind it, separated by a small patio, is the cooking, bathing, and toilet area. Upstairs is one big sleeping area, no beds. This is all right because we only have one mat and one mosquito net. This place is used by the rice planters during rice-planting season, and by the harvesters during the harvest.

Life is peaceful. There are lots of wild chickens, plenty of running water, and sacks of rice hidden in a tiny hut at the end of a small rice field nearby. Once in a while some of the men leave for town very early in the morning and return with marinated and salted freshly killed pigs and fish, and news.

The Japanese are marching forward following the retreating U.S. and Philippine forces and are committing atrocities against the civilians they come across. Women, children, old people, and the sick are not spared. The men report about an eleven-year-old girl who died of bleeding after she was brutally raped by five Japanese soldiers. So, Father gets everybody on the alert and posts watchers.

Tatay Iboy teaches Tommy and me to use the slingshot (a Y-shaped piece of strong and sturdy wood with one end of strong elastics attached to the tip of the Y and joined together at the other end by a piece of leather for the stone). We each have one, mine is bigger for bigger stones. We have target practices till we are good at hitting them from a long distance as well. He says, "Used properly and successfully, it would be effective in giving you time to run and escape."

So Tommy and I go around with our pockets always full of stones, but not big ones that weigh us down and slow us if we have to run. Sometimes I carry Tommy piggyback, running everywhere, while Tommy shoots at targets.

Tatay Iboy is also training *Ate* Nene and me in handling and using a *balisong*—a small double-edged three-inch switchblade knife. We each have one. We practice using a banana plant as the target and learn how to inflict most damage in defending ourselves and Tommy. Because we are small and can not reach the heart or neck, *Tatay* Iboy tells us to stab toward the groin, the inguinal region, and slash upward and out. We practice daily to develop strength and accuracy. *Tatay* Iboy is an expert knife wielder and fighter; he comes from Batangas, a province well-known for having the best knife fighters. He and Father believe that it is better for us to die fighting and taking with us or damaging as many as possible than to be captured alive to suffer constant multiple rapes and other tortures and eventually die from them.

One day, one of the posted watchers runs into the clearing shouting "*japon, japon*" and he runs into the forest followed by most of the men. My grandfather, always armed with a sheathed long double-edge combat knife (*punyal*) and a hatchet hanging at his belt, also disappears taking *Ate* Nene with him. They not only are avoiding capture but also taking defensive positions and guaranteeing survivors should there be a massacre.

Through the small opening in the thicket, two Japanese soldiers emerge into the clearing and walk toward some older people sitting on benches around a picnic table. The soldiers talk to them, all the time smiling, and our people shrug and shake their heads. Father, with me following, approaches the two soldiers, shakes hands, and asks them to sit down. One is older and shorter, but both look nice and friendly. The taller, younger one who has a gun at one side and a sheathed knife on the other, sits on a big rock, while Father and the older one, who also has a gun on one side and a long sheathed saber on the other, take the only two empty chairs. The older people around the table do not leave. The older Japanese soldier says in good English but with a strong accent, "We are separated from our unit and are lost. Please give direction to town."

After Father gives him directions, the soldier says, "I am a philosophy professor at the University of Tokyo, but now a colonel in the army. The younger one [looking and pointing to the young Japanese soldier] is an engineering student at the same university and now a lieutenant."

As they talk, the younger one looks at me and smiles. He takes out his dictionary, looks at it and says, "hello little sister" and beckons with his head for me to come closer, pointing at his dictionary. Curious, I approach and look at the dictionary. I can read the English part; the others are not words but characters of lines crossing each other in different ways. I look at him and ask, "What is that?" and he says, "*kanji*, Japanese writing."

Then he takes out his wallet, and shows me pictures of his parents and of a smiling little girl about my age. He points to her, looks in the dictionary, and says, "my sister, same you, miss her."

When they stand up to leave, both face Father and me, click their heels together and bow from the waist and say something that sounds like "*arigato gozaimash*."

Everybody relaxes when they leave; *Tatay* Iboy and *Ate* Nene come back, but Tommy is nowhere in sight and everyone asks about him. I tell them, "I know where he might be." and I run to a clump of thick bushes near a stand of trees.

We used to hide there during target practice and pelt different targets from there. I call out when I don't see him among the bushes. Then I hear him say "*ate*" from above. I look up and he is straddling a branch slightly behind the trunk of a tree, his slingshot in one hand. We have gotten very good at climbing trees with low hanging branches, even three-year-old Tommy. His problem is getting down. So I stand nearer to the tree; he puts his slingshot back in his belt, turns around and slowly lowers himself while his arms and small hands with the strong grip hold on to the branch. I reach up to grab his legs and guide his feet to my shoulders. Then he lets go of the branch and grabs my hands. I lower myself and help him jump down. As we walk back I ask, "What are you doing up the tree?"

He says, "I'm aiming at the young soldier's head ready to pelt him if he should touch and carry you off." At that distance he would not miss. My brave little hero.

A Taste of Tragedy

The men no longer go to town for our supply of pork and fish. They say it is getting dangerous; the Japanese occupy the town and forage for food as well. They do not want to lead them to us. Sometimes we can hear shootings from far off.

Because we eat the wild chickens before they can lay eggs, and eat the eggs before they can hatch, food is beginning to get scarce. Then Tiyeng discovers snails in the mud at the bottom of the stream. With the help of Tommy and *Ate* Nene, she comes out with a pail full. I stay on the banks and watch because I am afraid of going into the water and being swept away. She washes them in the stream and then soaks them in salted water overnight so that they will spit out the mud, according to her. The next morning, she drains and washes them and then boils them in diluted vinegar, crushed garlic, salt, sliced ginger, chopped onions, and some vegetables. We pull the meat out with a toothpick and eat them with our rice and drink the broth. They are delicious.

We are awakened one morning by cannon shelling; some of them dropping and exploding some distance beyond the rice field, some closer. Father says, "They seem to be random shooting rather than in a definite pattern. That is more dangerous; one cannot gauge its direction."

Our people decide to build a bomb shelter. They dig a long and wide ditch, beneath some trees, and cover it with a roof made of strong interlacing split bamboo covered with *nipa* and palm leaves interwoven among interlacing pieces of wood, top this with layers of mounds of earth, mud, and stones. It is deep enough for people to sit comfortably and move around slightly stooped. They leave an opening at one end where one person can go in and out easily. Inside they put jars of water, food, blankets, and pillows. The shelter is big enough for several families. Some of the women and children sleep there at night.

In our hut, Father and *Tatay* Iboy move our sleeping quarters from the second floor to downstairs; Mother and the children (*Ate* Nene, Tommy, Rey, and I) under the big and heavy rough dining table. Tiyeng, Father, and *Tatay* Iboy sleep separately under or surrounded by the other furniture.

One afternoon, after a session of shelling, one of the young men runs to Father saying, "*Tata* Enteng (one of Mother's cousins) was hit while threshing the palay (unhusked grain of rice). He told me to come get you."

So Father, with me tagging along, follows the young man to the hut where they have placed *Tata* Enteng on a *papag* (bed made of split-bamboo). He is moaning and once in a while he screams. When he sees Father, he asks him, "Tom, take your gun (Father has a small revolver) and shoot me. I am dying slowly and painfully and I cannot stand the pain anymore. I feel this hot, burning knife cutting through my insides."

Father does not say anything. He looks at the wound on the right side just below the ribs; it is small and hardly bleeding. He takes his flashlight and peers into the wound. *Tata* Enteng is perspiring heavily and grits his teeth and a trickle of blood appears. Then he gags and more blood comes out. Father wipes the blood off with a small towel, gives him water to drink when he asks for it. Then he gags more blood out again and weakly begs Father to shoot him. Father takes hold of *Tata* Enteng's chin with his left hand and his right fist delivers an uppercut punch to *Tata* Enteng's jaw knocking him out; Father is a champion amateur boxer in his district of Binondo. He washes his hands at the sink.

As we walk back I ask him, "why did you hit *Tata* Enteng?"

"He is dying; I tried to see if I can find the shrapnel and pull it out so that he would bleed normally and not internally and probably give him a chance of surviving. It is too deep inside, and he would die slowly, painfully. Knocking him out and rendering him unconscious saves him from the suffering and he can die peacefully." *Tata* Enteng dies at dusk without waking up.

A Touch of Irony

One morning I wake up to several voices talking. I look out and see Father talking to a Filipino soldier. I wash up, have breakfast, and join Father. They are Philippine Scouts, highly trained fighters and expert sharpshooters, trained by and connected with the U.S. army, bringing up the rear of the retreating army. They decide to set up a line of defense by us, across the stream and by the rice field. They are not all bunched up at one place. They are scattered all around in small groups. They dig "foxholes" (ditches just big enough for one person to move around in and deep enough for the person to sit in it completely out of sight or kneel and shoot out of). They do not approve of our bomb shelter.

At the Commander's orders, they dig a foxhole for Father and another slightly bigger one for Tommy and me near our house. Tommy and I have so much fun jumping in and out of it and target practicing with our slingshot. Of course I have to pull Tommy out or push him up so he can get out. Father and the Commander are always talking with each other. With the Scouts' presence around us, we feel safe from Japanese intrusion.

After breakfast one morning, a barrage of shelling suddenly starts and one passes with a loud hissing sound over our settlement, exploding loudly not too far behind. I am reading in our living room and Tommy is playing outside. I jump up, snatch a pillow, grab him, and race toward our foxhole while shouting to Mother, *Ate* Nene, and Tiyeng, "Take shelter under the table; you don't have time to go to the bomb shelter."

Tatay Iboy and some of the men have gone deeper into the forest early this morning to hunt for wild hogs. Father, who is talking to the Commander, runs to the house to check on Mother and the rest, then comes out and goes to his foxhole after checking on Tommy and me. The Commander has gone to join his men. All the others are running toward the shelter.

The barrage continues, again dropping randomly. I am half-way kneeling, peeking out; Tommy is slightly standing, slingshot ready aimed. Suddenly there is the loud hissing sound of a passing shell. I pull Tommy down and put the pillow on top of him and hunker down with him. A very loud explosion sounds somewhere behind us. This is followed immediately by a louder but shorter hissing sound and a deafening explosion. That one is very close, may even be in our compound. A few more random shelling and then quiet.

Father gets out of his foxhole, checks on us, and looks at our hut. He heaves a sigh of relief when he sees it standing and unharmed. I go in; Mother and the rest are still under the table over which Father has piled pillows and blankets, and arranged the long benches and chairs around it like a wall.

The Commander and some of his men come running toward us saying "you took a direct hit." They walk and look around and see the other huts also intact. Then they walk toward the shelter and see smoke coming out of it. It has suffered the direct hit; the top is blown out, the shell going through the opening hitting the back of the oldest woman in our midst as she entered the shelter, and exploding inside. Everyone inside is killed except for a baby who is saved by its mother's body over it; but it can not hear.

Tatay Iboy and the other men arrive and rush to the scene. The smell of the explosion hurts my nose. It is decided that the bodies will stay and be buried there. The Scouts help in throwing the earth into the ditch. The deaths diminish our population to one-third, which includes us and the hog hunters. What irony! That which is meant to shelter and save is now a grave.

The following morning, the remainder of our people talk about going deeper into the forests and jungles. Some of them say, "We may possibly join guerrilla groups that are starting to form in several parts of Bataan, now that our women, children, the elderly . . . our families . . . are gone." The baby's father and his sister who has been washing clothes upstream during the raid decide to look for and join another settlement.

The Commander tells Father, "The Japanese are closing in and so we are being forced to retreat to Mariveles, a town across Corregidor, to make our last stand. The reinforcement of men and ammunition we are waiting for is not forthcoming."

When Father says that we would go with them, the Commander says, "No, attorney, we won't be able to protect you. We don't have enough supplies and ammunition, but I can assure you that every bullet out of every gun in this unit will find a Japanese target. And if that is gone, we will do hand combat and take down as many as we can. I suggest that you go back to Manila, it has been occupied for a while now and it is calm. You're city folks and would not last long in the jungles, especially since there are children."

Then he gives Father, *Ate* Nene, and me a water canteen each and shows my aunt and Mother how to make a backpack. This idea of a backpack is good; it allows both hands and arms to be free.

He says, "we'll leave soon after you leave. Be sure to travel early morning and most of day; never at night because that's when they send out patrols. Watch out for reconnaissance planes and troop convoys on the highway; stay under cover of trees. If you have to flee from someone with a gun, run in a zig-zag and when you hear that snap, dive and crawl away as fast as you can before getting up. Good luck." And he shakes my Father's hand.

A Sharp Birdlike Whistle

That afternoon we pack and store food and water. We leave at dawn the next morning. Tommy has his own little backpack filled with a change of clothes and a face towel; his wooden shoes, tied together, hang on one strap of the pack. His slingshot is tucked in his belt, his pockets filled with stones. He carries his small pillow in one arm.

My backpack is a large pillow case tied at each end with a rope and this into loops as shoulder straps. In addition to my two clothes changes, I carry two towels, another set of clothes for Tommy and some diapers for Rey. My wooden shoes hang on one strap of the pack, like Tommy's, and my canteen filled with fresh spring water hangs on the other pack strap. My slingshot is also tucked in my belt, one pocket filled with stones, and the other has my switchblade.

Tommy, *Ate* Nene, and I put on our soft rubber shoes which we put away after that first walking trip; we have been using wooden shoes since. They are comfortable, flexible, and keep our feet protected. All of us have backpacks, except Mother who carries baby Rey supported by a diaper sling around her neck, and *Tatay* Iboy who has balanced on his shoulders a split bamboo pole, strong and flexible, with a gasoline can at each end. One is filled with water, the other with rice, salt, and some cooked food. *Tatay* Iboy is slightly built but strong, wiry, and quick.

The adults decide to take a shorter route to town because of our limited food and water supply and the wear and tear on the children and Mother. On this route we have to wade across the stream where it is wider and deeper and cross two highways and the expansive and open rice fields on either side of them, but it will cut the trip down by three days.

I dread crossing the stream; I am imagining Edgar Allan Poe's "The Maelstrom." When I hesitate on the banks, Tommy comes back for me, holds my hand and guides me. The water is up to my knees and to Tommy's waistline. My heart is pounding with every step but Tommy holds on tightly and pulls me. His fearlessness and determination get me across.

When we get to the edge of the first rice field from the cover of trees, the plan is not to run as a group, but in stages: first *Tatay* Iboy and *Ate* Nene to run across the field and up onto the highway, cross it and down to the other rice field and run to the cover of trees at the end of the field; then Tommy and I, followed by Father guiding and supporting Mother and the baby, and last Tiyeng. Tatay Iboy will leave his pack with *Ate* Nene, give three birdlike whistles to let us know they have reached safety and signal the next to start running across. He will run back toward the highway to meet and help the next ones. If there is danger, he will give one sharp bird whistle and two for all clear. And if we are somewhere in the middle of the field, we are to drop down and pretend to be dead.

He and *Ate* Nene reach the safety of the trees on the other side and he signals for me and Tommy to start. Crossing the field is difficult because it is not flat; it is pockmarked by the dry rice paddies that require jumping down into it, running across and jumping up on the other side, then repeating the whole thing until the last one. I hold Tommy's free hand to help him jump in and out. When we are about one fourth in, *Tatay* Iboy whistles sharply once. Tommy and I quickly run back to the trees, father runs to meet us and scoops Tommy up. A convoy of several trucks of Japanese troops rumbles into view. We watch and wonder if *Tatay* Iboy is back in the safety of the trees or somewhere in the middle of the field.

With the all-clear signal, Tommy and I run as fast as we can. Now that we know how to hurdle the paddies, it is much easier. When we reach the edge of the highway, *Tatay* Iboy is already up there. To help Tommy up the embankment, I make him go back a few steps, then run fast and up without stopping and I sort of helped by pulling him up by the arm and then letting go and pushing him up. *Tatay* Iboy then reaches down to pull him up and gives him a little push across the highway, then turns to give me a hand. Father and Mother are already crossing the field as I run down the other side of the embankment toward the trees.

We sleep soundly that evening after a light meal of cold rice and fried marinated chicken pieces because we can not risk building a fire to cook. We drink the water from the big can. The canteen water is being saved for emergency. We get up very early dawn to start the walk. We cross the rice field between two heavy stands of trees before the second highway without any trouble. That saves us time to stop and rest early. *Tatay* Iboy finds a spring where we sponge bathe and soak hot, tired legs and feet. That night is not peaceful. In the shelter of our trees, we hear but not see lots of activities—gunshots, trucks rumbling, airplanes. The sleeping mat is not laid out in full, just enough for Mother, the baby, Tommy, *Ate* Nene, and me. The mosquito net is torn and shredded in some parts and so it is just draped over us. Father, *Tatay* Iboy, and Tiyeng are up and on the alert, each one taking turns dozing off.

We get up earlier than usual because we are eagerly anticipating getting into town soon for proper shelter, food and water—only one more highway to cross. As the rest of us stand in the shelter of the last stand of trees, *Tatay* Iboy and *Ate* Nene successfully cross the highway and make it safely to the other side. Tommy and I start to race across the rice paddies when we hear *Tatay* Iboy's one whistle warning. We are in the middle of the rice field, no time to run back to the safety of the trees or go forward to the shelter of the dike. So I tell Tommy to drop down and hug his pillow, and I lie down almost on top of him hugging him under me, not only to protect him, but also to cover up any possible wiggling or movement.

We hear the sound of airplanes; Tommy complains about a horrible stench that I also smell and I see a dead, decomposing Japanese soldier at the other end of the rice paddy. I tell Tommy to bury his nose in the pillow so he wouldn't sneeze as the airplane sound gets louder and closer. The planes, three of them, slow down, circle above us, and seem to fly lower. We hold our breath; the planes fly away. We are ready to get up but have not heard *Tatay* Iboy's all-clear signal. After a short while the drone of an airplane hits us. Apparently one of them decides to come back and recheck the scene. Several long minutes later we hear the all-clear signal, get up and begin running; Father and Mother and the baby right behind us and not too far behind is Tiyeng. We make it safely to the shelter of the trees on the other side as a convoy of Japanese trucks rumbles down the highway.

Later, Father says, "It's a good thing that you waited for *Tatay* Iboy's signal, because if the pilot, who came back, found you in a different position or location, he would have strafed you."

We stay behind as *Tatay* Iboy and *Ate* Nene emerge from the shelter of the tree and go toward town. He returns with *Tata* Julian, *Kuya* Ipe, and *Nana* Ana. *Tata* Julian picks up and carries Tommy, *Nana* Ana takes baby Rey from Mother, and *Kuya* Ipe (big, young, and strong) carries Mother. We go to the house of *Nana* Guida (*Kuya* Ipe's mother and *Nana* Ana's older sister, and my grandmother's first cousins) because my grandparents' house (the biggest and sturdiest in the town) is now the house and office of the commander of the small Japanese garrison. The Japanese have also taken over the granary and converted it to barracks. They left the fish ponds and the home industry of poultry, piggery, and truck gardens untouched. But they demand a lot of the harvests.

Nana Guida's house is big enough and comfortable. It feels good to have a nice, long, bath, hot food, fresh cool water to drink, and a warm and soft bamboo bed covered with clean sheets and pillows.

However, after several days, it is decided that we cannot stay there very long; we need to leave before we attract the attention of the Japanese and be brought to the garrison for questioning. Moreover, Father starts having attacks of malaria—first, several long minutes of teeth-chattering chills that cannot be helped by thick blankets or hot teas or soups, then followed by a very high fever for hours that makes him delirious and very weak after it is over. He needs medicine and medical attention badly. We need to get to Manila or some place where there are doctors.

Traveling by land is impossible without transportation, even just to the border of Pampanga, (Father says about 70+ kilometers). Moreover, it is dangerous because of sporadic skirmishes and shelling throughout the rest of Bataan and the presence of so many Japanese soldiers. So we have to go by water—cross Manila Bay from the shores of Mabatang to the shores of Malolos, the capital of the province of Bulacan. Not only is it a big town with a hospital, but it is also the closest province to Manila. It is a very risky move because the water is part of the Pacific Ocean and the bay is full of Japanese war ships and patrol boats.

A Refugee Camp

At four o'clock on a dark, cloudy morning of March 1942, we board a small one-outrigger *banca* (a fishing boat shaped like a canoe), outfitted with a bright oil lamp on a pole at the front end and another one at the rear end. We cross at the narrowest point. All of us children are wearing dark clothing. At the front of the boat, sits *Tatay* Iboy holding an oar in each hand and below him on another wooden plank across the width of the boat sits Tiyeng disguised as a pregnant woman. Below their seats lies *Ate* Nene under some fishing nets.

In the middle of the boat, the boatman has placed thermos and pots and other household things and other fishing gears in plain view. In the rear, sits Mother with baby Rey in her arms and next to her sits Father all hunched up with a light wrap across his shoulders, and a little above them sits the boatman with another set of oars. Below their seats lie Tommy and me under nets.

We can see the lights of the battle ships afar as they move around slowly, and the crisscrossing lights of the faster-moving patrol boats. Midway between the two shores, a Japanese patrol boat starts approaching us and shining a bright searchlight into the boat I tell Tommy to face the back of the boat and close his eyes because they will reflect the light. Their leader addresses the boatman who tells him, "I am taking my pregnant wife (pointing to Tiyeng) to see a doctor because she is having difficulty, and the old man (pointing to *Tatay* Iboy) is her father."

They shine the light on each person when identified. Then, pointing to Mother, he says, "She is the sister of my wife with a sick baby who needs to go to the hospital and next to her is her husband who is suffering from malaria."

Suddenly, the light is turned off and the boat pulls away fast and the leader gruffly tells the boatman to go on his way. When they are gone, the boatman chuckles and says, "Now we know what to mention to keep these devils away from us." When *Tatay* Iboy asks what, he says, "malaria."

Father says, "that stands to reason. It is very contagious. A sting from a mosquito that just stung a malaria sufferer can cause an epidemic. And on the water, there are lots and lots of mosquitoes."

When we reach the Malolos shore, a group of people come to meet us and help us out of the boat into dry land. Then, someone who seems to be the leader takes us to one of the houses by the shore; these houses sit on stilts. He shows us up the outside stairs into a big living room and points to one corner closest to the door and says,

> This is where you'll be staying. We've had so many refugees. As you can see the other three corners are already taken. There's a cooking and eating area to the side and a bathing area, too. At the back of the house is an outhouse, and here are two padlock keys to it.

He hands one each to *Tatay* Iboy and Tiyeng.

Two men come to string up two privacy dividers made of big sheets. One side is partly folded up in the daytime and let down at night. The place is clean and big enough to be comfortable, but no beds. We sleep on woven mats laid out on the floor at night and have a mosquito net over us. It is really better than sleeping out in the open fields.

Father's malaria attacks come frequently, every other day now, and he is left very weak after each bout. Then Mother and Tiyeng come down with dysentery. Some old folk healers tell them to drink the liquid from either boiled guava leaves or corn silk to wash off the impurities. That seems to help, but sometimes I see them double up in pain, even when they are lying down. It is worse for Mother because she is pregnant. When this happens, and Rey starts fussing and crying, I pick him up and go downstairs. I cradle him on my lap or bounce him on my knees as I sit on the last step of the ladder watching Tommy play. We, the children, are told not to eat or touch any food or drink coming from others or that has not been boiled.

Tatay Iboy helps out in the kitchen at the hospital, a three-story building, which he says is so full that the sick are sleeping on the floor of the hallways. There are only nine real nurses; the others are volunteers. There are only four doctors. The only things he asks of them are quinine tablets for Father, some pills to relieve dysentery, and good drinking water.

To add to Mother's pain, baby Rey starts getting sick and is in a bad shape; he just lies there, not sleeping, not crying, not eating. Now and then, Mother soaks a corner of a boiled face towel in the liquid of boiled rice and with her finger runs it around his mouth just to give him liquid.

One day, a young couple, whose medical studies at the University of the Philippines were cut off on their last year by the war, comes to visit us; they have been making the rounds of the refugee camps. They give Father more quinine pills, aspirin for fever, and some pills for Mother and Tiyeng. When the lady medical intern sees Rey and is told of his condition, she concludes that he has severe indigestion, probably from eating adult food before his little body could take it. Now he is dehydrated and starving and would slowly die.

She tells my Mother and Father, "I'll try something drastic as a last resort; it might help but it will not do harm or make it worse. Will you let me do it?"

And they give her permission. The lady tells Tiyeng, “Could you please boil some lightly-sugared water.”

When this has cooled down she takes some into a syringe and injects it slowly into Rey’s stomach. She does it again the next two days. Rey starts to improve; he begins to cry and to drink boiled rice liquid with a little salt. On the third day, she injects the sugared water into his thigh saying, “I do not want to interrupt the returning natural activity of the stomach but still want to give him nutrition.”

Rey starts to eat soft food, like mashed up boiled rice and yam. When he starts bowel movements, then the lady doctor believes he is on his way to healing. My parents are very relieved and appreciative. Father gives her our address in Manila and says, “Please come visit us when this is all over, and we are all back home in Manila.”

A Refugee Situation Ends

Sitting on that last ladder step, one morning, watching Tommy play, I see a car going slowly down the street. *Ate* Nene sees it too and she runs toward it and knocks on the door, shouting “stop! stop!”, but the car does not stop. So she runs in front of it where the driver can see her, stops, and waves her hands. I run toward the car and bang on the door, signaling to Tommy to stay away. The car stops and the driver comes out and strides angrily toward *Ate* Nene. *Ate* Nene stands her ground and I stand beside her. I see that she has her hand in her pocket that holds the switchblade knife. I come closer to her and whisper, “No, *Ate* Nene, he is not a Japanese. We can talk to him.” *Ate* Nene, like *Tatay* Iboy, is very brave and quick, but she has a fiery temper and tends to be rash.

Before the driver can come close to us, an elderly, kind-looking man comes out of the back seat, followed by a younger man. The older man approaches us and asks kindly, “Now little girls, what do you want?”

Ate Nene says, “We need help; we are not from here; we have to get home to Manila for the family doctor. Her father is sick (pointing to me); her mother and my other sister are also sick and so is her baby brother.”

At this point Tommy comes over and holds my hand. The man says, "I would like to help you but I cannot because if I do that I will have to help everyone here and that is impossible."

Ate Nene insists, "but her father needs medical help. He is important."

The man smiles and turns to me and asks, "Now, little girl, what is your father's name?"

I answer, "Tomas Yumol."

His eyes widen and he says, "Tom?" I nod my yes. He continues, "Attorney Tomas Yumol?"

And I answer "yes, sir."

He turns to the younger man and says, "Now, why was I not informed of this? Why didn't anybody tell me?"

The young man says, "we didn't know about it, sir."

Then he turns to me and asks, "why didn't your father come to see me. He knows where I live."

"Sir, he has malaria and is very weak after every attack; he sometimes cannot stand up and walk around."

He looks at Tommy and asks, "and this little boy . . . ?"

I answer, "he is Tommy, Jr. sir."

He bends down and picks up Tommy and carries him on one arm and his other hand takes hold of mine and he says, "okay, take me to him."

When we reach the top of the stairs and turn toward our spot, the older man puts Tommy down and comes closer to Father, who is slightly reclining on two pillows against the wall, his eyes closed. The man softly calls out Father's name. Father does not respond, so the man calls out loudly, "Tom."

Father opens his eyes, looks at the man and says, "Governor!" and he tries to sit up, but the Governor bends and touches his shoulder and tells him not to, as he squats next to Father.

Father asks, "what are you doing here?"

The Governor answers, "your two little smart girls (patting both our heads) brought me. Why did you not let me know that you are here?"

Father responds, "the malaria attacks leave me so weak to even get out of the house."

The Governor says, "but you could have sent someone, even your smart little girls."

Then the Governor says, "I'm taking you and your family to my house, get medical attention and start healing. I owe you that much. Then you can decide what you want to do; you can be my legal adviser, or pick up your practice here, or go back to Manila."

Ate Nene runs to the hospital to tell *Tatay* Iboy.

We try to get into his car but we cannot all fit in. *Tatay* Iboy says he will walk and *Ate* Nene and I decide to walk with him. Tommy tries to get out of the car to join us, but I tell him, "Stay in the car and watch Rey." I feel so light and happy I start skipping instead of just walking.

After four days of medical attention from the Governor's personal doctor, adequate medicine, and good food and rest, Father feels well and strong enough to be able to travel to Manila. So do my Mother and Tiyeng. The Governor and the doctor tell them to take two more days. The Governor lends us his *carretela* (horse-drawn carriage that can take more than three passengers because it has one additional three-passenger seat behind the driver's). So very early this morning, we start our long way back to Manila.

A Small Step toward Normalcy

The road is not full of traffic. The driver tells us that we will have to stop at three sentry points. At the first one, two Japanese guards approach us and look into the *carretela* and ask questions of the driver. He shows them a piece of paper and the guards signal us to go on.

We arrive in a small town at lunch time and the driver takes us to a roadside house that has an eating place on the first floor. We all get down to eat, except Father and Mother who still feel weak and tired, so Tiyeng buys food and drinks for them to eat in the *carretela*.

The same thing happens at the other two sentry points; two guards approach and look into the *carretela*, asks questions and the driver shows them the letter, and they tell us to go on. *Tatay* Iboy observes, "We seem to be let by quicker than the other carriages."

The driver shows him the paper that he shows the guards; it is an official document signed by the Governor and by a Japanese in *Kanji* (like that in the young Japanese's dictionary) that says we are the Governor's visiting relatives and are on our way home to Manila.

When we arrive in Manila, *Tatay* Iboy says to Father and Mother, "Let us go to our house first instead of yours and stay there until you are stronger. Berto's family—his mother, the cook; his older brother, the all around handyman; his sister and sister-in-law, the clothes washers and house cleaners—will be there because they decided to stay to look after the house and not evacuate. Everyone will be able to rest well, especially you two, who will have all the help you need."

Tatay Iboy's house is in Valderrama, in the Binondo District. When we arrive we see that all the streets that bounded the big house, which sits in the middle of a one-block square, are closed off, fenced, and guarded by Japanese sentries armed with rifles and bayonets. According to the neighbors, the house is now occupied by the Japanese commander as residence and office. The piggery, the poultry, and the orchard are gone.

All of Berto's relatives have moved to a smaller house several streets away carrying with them some valuables from *Tatay* Iboy's house that they have been able to save before the Japanese takeover of the house. They are ready to hand them over to *Tatay* Iboy and Tiyeng once they get settled.

So we go instead to *Lola* Sabel's (Father's mother) residence (a rented two-story, two-bedroom townhouse, like ours) in San Nicolas, not far from Valderama, in the same district. In this house live, besides *Lola* Sabel, Father's younger sister, *Tya* (Aunt) Anchang and her young son, and their youngest brother, *Tyo* Tenyong. *Kuya* Turing, oldest son of their older brother, *Tyo* Dadong, who lives in Zamboanga, one of the provinces in the big island of Mindanao, southernmost part of the Philippines, is also staying there while he goes to the university. It is kind of crowded but better than the refugee house in Malolos. *Tatay* Iboy tells his brother-in-law, *Lolo* Anong about the situation and he invites him, Tiyeng, and *Ate* Nene to stay in his home.

When Father feels stronger and is no longer having frequent malaria attacks, he decides to go to our townhouse in Cataluna (pronounced "Catalunia"), Sampaloc District, far from San Nicolas, and check its condition. *Tatay* Iboy and *Tyo* Tenyong accompany him; they take a *calesa* (horse-drawn three-passenger carriage) because there are no cars, taxis, or buses because the Japanese have commandeered them all. When he returns, he says, "The house is okay; Mr. Villa and the other neighbors who did not leave, have been watching it. The neighborhood is intact."

So we pack our belongings again and return to our townhouse. *Ate* Nene joins us.

As soon as we feel settled, Mother calls our family doctor, Dr. Prospero. He comes one morning and checks everyone out; first Mother and her growing pregnancy and status of her rheumatism, then Father and his malaria—gives him more quinine, and aspirin for fever, and suggests good nutrition and rests—then *Ate* Nene, me, and Tommy, all of whom he finds healthy. He examines ten-month old Rey and notices a big soft lump along his right thigh, like a huge blister. He touches it and presses down on it without getting any reaction from Rey. So he concludes it is not infected or inflamed. My parents tell him what that young doctor at the refugee center did to keep Rey alive. He approves of it and says,

> That was good thinking and a daring move, but effective. On the thigh, after some injections of the fluid subcutaneously, the liquid failed to be absorbed and so is accumulated under the skin. I will have to make a small incision and drain it out.

He washes the wound out with saline solution. Then he prescribes "Agua de Vichy" as a strengthening tonic and intestinal cleaner.

Japanese Occupation: January 1942– February 1945

How the Victors Treat the Conquered

One afternoon, Mr. and Mrs. Villa and some of Father's chess mates visit us bringing homemade lemonade and homemade rice cookies. Mr. Villa tells Father,

> Tom, since January 4 (1942), the University of Santo Tomas has been closed to public access. It has been converted to an interment camp for thousands of non-military Americans living in the Philippines, after the successful Japanese entry and occupation of Manila on January 2 (1942). The whole huge and sprawling campus, except for the church area, is taken up.

Every Catholic student in every Catholic school knows that the University of Santo Tomas is the largest and oldest university in Asia and in the Philippines. It is a Catholic University established in 1611 by the Dominican Mission from Spain in the sixteenth century.

Of the three high cement walls surrounding the campus, at the back and two sides, there is a double iron-gated entrance on each side wall, one facing Gov. Forbes street and the other P. Noval street, two streets from ours. The front, facing Espana Boulevard, a major street, has a cement wall, half in height of the other three, topped by beautiful wrought iron bars. Now there is a big notice close to the front gate declaring it to be be an internment camp. These are now covered with thick straw mats for privacy and topped by barb wire. The front gate, the main entrance to the campus, located midway, is very wide allowing for two-way motor vehicle traffic; it has a wide double iron gate.

The side entrance on Gov. Forbes and the front main one on Espana are guarded, day and night; the one on the side is guarded by one fully armed sentry inside the closed locked gate, and the one in front by two on the outside. The front main gates are closed but not locked to allow access for Japanese military business. The side entrance on P. Noval leads to the church and is accessible to the public. However, the grounds in front of the church, as well as in the back and on one side are totally closed off from the main campus by a tall sturdy wooden fence without any gates. There are many stories of unspeakable hardships, deprivation, beatings, and unexplained deaths behind those walls.

On April 9 (1942), a month after our escape from Bataan and a day after Tommy's fourth birthday, Bataan falls to the Japanese. It has been talked about that the American and Filipino soldiers who surrendered are marched a long way to a concentration camp. The fully armed Japanese ride trucks, motorcycles, and cars. According to witness reports, this march is full of horrendous sufferings: deprivation of food, water, and sleep, and beatings of those who slow down the march. The marching soldiers suffer all kinds of illnesses such as fever, malaria, dysentery. Those who are too weak to stand up and walk and slow down the march are bayoneted on the spot and left to die. And so are those who try to help them. After the marching line and Japanese trucks have passed out of view, some townspeople come and retrieve the bodies of the fallen soldiers and bury those who do not survive and care for those who do. These, later on, join the guerrilla movement. The people start referring to that march as a "death march."

On May 5 (1942), a week before Rey's birthday, Corregidor falls and General Jonathan Wainwright surrenders all of the American troops. This marks the fall of the Philippines to the Japanese.

How the Whole Country Is Controlled

To control the population and govern the country, a Philippine government has been set up. The rule of Philippine President Manuel L. Quezon, who was evacuated to the United States at the start of the invasion, as president of a government in exile, ended when the Philippines fell to Japan. Dr. Jose P. Laurel, whom he left in charge, has been officially appointed president by Tokyo to head the new government. He answers to the Japanese high command and so the people call the government a "puppet government." The Japanese, in turn, deals with him on matters of national peace and order and does not bother with us. So we hardly see Japanese soldiers on the streets.

Any criminal activity is handled by the local police, brought to court, is resolved, and not allowed to reach the Japanese command, which would not care who is guilty and who is not and will punish both parties severely and cruelly.

In Manila, to control the vast population, the Japanese order the formation of neighborhood associations consisting of residents of three adjacent streets. Each association is to handle all kinds of problems within its neighborhood. It reports to the puppet government through a neighborhood-selected representative.

With Father back, the neighbors decide to formally form our neighborhood association consisting of our street, Cataluna and the one on either side of it, Adelina (to the right of us) and Eloisa (to the left). But because P. Noval, the street bounding one side of the University of Santo Tomas, and adjacent to Eloisa, is left alone, its residents decide to join us. On our street we have two doctors, a dentist, two pharmacists, several engineers, an architect, successful businessmen, a congressman, and teachers. The residents of the four streets unanimously elect my Father as president and select the congressman as neighborhood representative to the puppet government.

In anticipation of the possibility of a growing scarcity of food, Father decides that the first need is to set up a food co-op and assigns *Aling* (honorific title for any nonrelative woman) Taleh's neighborhood store to be the central storage of large amounts of staples like rice, yams, beans, salt, sugar, canned milk, and so on to be bought wholesale from a big warehouse set up by the Japanese once a month. Each household contributes what it can for these big purchases. Mr. S. who owns a very large rice plantation in Nueva Ecija, a rice-growing province North of Manila, sets aside sacks of rice before the Japanese come to collect the harvest and donates two large sacks to the co-op. Another resident, a sugar baron from the South, also donates sacks of his sugar harvest to the co-op. Then the supplies, as needed, are retailed off to the residents. The Japanese commander in charge of the warehouse learns of our co-op and approves of it.

One day, our neighborhood association decides to have a fund-raising drive. They sell tickets to the other neighborhoods for a dance and refreshment evening at the cafeteria of one of the neighboring public schools. It is very festive and the different bits of refreshment are prepared by our resident. and donated to the function. The residents from the other neighborhoods get to know our residents; they talk, they dance, they eat, and they laugh and have a good time. We, the children, are allowed in as long as we behave.

The Japanese commander in our area and his aides are invited; they watch the dance and eat some refreshment. Father and the officers of the association talk to the commander and his aides. They seem to have a friendly conversation. The commander and his men do not stay long. Because the drive is successful, it is decided that there will be another one later in the year. And so our neighborhood is more well-off than most in the city and our residents are not going hungry or feeling deprived.

At the beginning of each month, the Japanese also hand out vouchers to each family, through the association, as permits to buy staples from a retail store they set up. This serves, for two days only, four neighborhood associations (twelve streets of approximately thirty homes per street). Residents who are in need of staples need to be there before the store closes. So this first time, early in the morning, Mother, *Ate* Nene, Tommy, and I go with some neighbors. We all approach the counter but two armed Japanese guards stop us and tell us to form a line.

"What? Form a line?" We, Filipinos, have never done this before. "So who goes first; who will be at the head of the line? And what will be the basis for that; age, gender, or social status?" And a discussion follows.

So, the Filipinos behind the counter, who will be helping out with the distribution, impatiently say, "You better just form a line and not waste time or the Japanese might just close the store."

Mother then tells everyone in our group, "let's have half of the adults be in front, the oldest and weakest to be first so as not to wait too long to be served, and half in the rear with the children in the middle where they can be controlled or protected."

As more people arrive, they are given the same information and the line gets longer. The guards walk up and down the line to keep order as people become restless because they are not accustomed to standing in line, and because of the sun's heat (umbrellas are not allowed) and the long wait as each person is served individually.

How a Slap Vindicates One's Dignity

One very hot summer day, we are lined up behind thirty people. A pretty young woman, about eighteen years old, somewhere in front of us, starts flirting and talking with a young guard, and the guard seems flattered and also talks and flirts with her. The line behind us starts getting restless and pushing. Mother, who is not very strong and is five months pregnant, gets pushed out of line. The guard turns and sees Mother as she tries to get back in line. So he angrily walks up to Mother, takes hold of her left arm and roughly pulls her out of line. Mother stumbles a little as her left foot slips out of her step-in, but her right arm swiftly swings up and delivers a loud and solid slap on the young guard's face. Before the surprised guard can react, she points a forefinger at his face, and with eyes blazing angrily, she tells him in a strong, steady voice,

> Call your commander so I can tell him that you are not doing your duty, not seeing the line becoming unruly and possibly turning into a riot, because you are flirting with a young woman. Go, call him, or I will have someone call him.

The young guard becomes pale, lets go of Mother's arm, and says, "no, no. Everything all right." Then he faces Mother, clicks his heels and bows low to her, saying, "so sorry, I not pay attention." Mother says, "all right" and the guard straightens up and walks away toward the rear. *Ate* Nene, who has been standing very close to the guard with her hand in her pocket that has her knife, relaxes and quietly moves away.

Mother now turns her attention to the young woman. She walks up to her and says, "Okay, you coquette! You shameless hussy! Does your mother know what you're doing, cheapening yourself like that in front of everybody? Is she here?"

The young woman bows her head, shaking it, and begins to cry silently. Then she gets out of line and starts to leave. Mother grabs her arm and says,

> Now, don't add stupidity to your indecency. Get back in line. You were sent here to get staples for your family and they are expecting this. You are going home empty-handed, and you will let them go hungry? What will you tell them? You already made one mistake. Don't add another. And next time you cannot control your 'itch' and want it scratched, do it somewhere where you will not cause anybody else any harm.

Then Mother looks at her and asks, "Where is your shopping bag?" She pulls a small one out of her pocket and shows it to Mother.

Mother says, "but that's too small. It can barely hold two kilos of rice and nothing more Where will you put the other staples?"

The young woman, sniffling, says, "I will buy only one kilo and the other staples, ma'am. That is enough for my mother, who washes clothes for others and gets some food, and me and my young crippled brother."

Mother turns to me and says, "Lita, give her you bag and you can have hers."

The young woman looks silently at the bag I give her, tears rolling down her cheeks. Mother then asks her, "How much money do you have?"

The young woman shows her. And when Mother sees how little, she gives the young woman some money and tells her, "Get two kilos plus the staples and some goodies for your brother."

The young woman, wiping her tears with the back of her hand, thanks Mother. Father, of course, hears the story, not just from Mother, but also from the neighbors.

How to Cool Down on a Hot Day

As the household elders get close and friendly in their common goal of survival and camaraderie, the children also become closer. Schools have not opened yet, so the children have all the time for play—tag, hide and seek, kick the can, skip rope, jump stick, run races, and *patintero* (a game of avoiding being tagged as one crosses a line on either side of a guard standing on the line, the one tagged gets to be the guard; best player is one who never gets tagged).

Our houses all border wide cement sidewalks; there are no front yards, even those non-townhouse styles (they have small enclosed yards between the back of the house and the kitchen as we have cemented patios). These sidewalks provide enough ground for our games. But sometimes, because there is hardly any traffic, our plays often spill into the streets, especially on those calm, clear, moonlit evenings. Even when it rains, we don't stay indoors. We are out there, playing, splashing in the rain. I still look out for Tommy as he plays with his friends of the same age. I stop my play, even if it is my turn, to attend to him when he gets hurt, which is not often because he is physically strong. Most of the time we play in front of our house because it is located about midway between Espana Boulevard, on one end of our street, and Isabelo de los Reyes Street, on the other end.

One warm day, as we are playing on the street, three Japanese soldiers, their bayonets sheathed to their sides, their rifles loosely held horizontally, walk by. We all stop playing and bow from the waist. The Japanese nod and walk on. Then they see the fire hydrant. They talk to each other, then they lay their rifles on the sidewalk, take off their caps with the white handkerchief like fabric hanging from them that covers their ears and back of their neck, and their uniforms down to their white g-strings. They open the hydrant, squat on the street, and take turns getting under the gushing water, talking and laughing.

Some parents approach us and tell us, "Children, isn't it time for your siestas? Go on home."

We stop our playing and go on to our respective homes. I tell Father about it and he says, "Next time that happens again, tell everyone quietly that it is time to go home for some chores."

This incident is discussed at the association's next meeting. Someone suggests that it be reported to the Japanese commander. Father says,

> I don't think that is a good idea. If they are not allowed to do that, those three soldiers will be punished severely. And to me that is not fair; they did no harm. They did not intend any harm; and they bothered no one. The fact that they put down their rifles on the sidewalk, making themselves vulnerable to attack, shows they trust us.

> They saw the fire hydrant as an opportunity to cool off. When they were done, they turned it off. Let us not try to aggravate them. The least they take notice of us, the better.

How Respect and Discipline Are Exacted

On May 24, 1942, I turn ten. There is no celebration as in previous birthdays, except an early morning mass at the University of Santo Tomas Church in a nice new dress that Tiyeng sewed and embroidered for me with a matching hair ribbon and a new pair of shoes given by my parents. Everyone says I look pretty in them and I am happy.

Then it is June. Schools begin enrollment. Because Sta. Isabel College is so far away, in Intramuros (the Spanish-walled city) across the Pasig River, and there is no school bus, my parents decide to enroll me and *Ate* Nene and Tommy (in pre-K) at a school closer to home. They select Instituto de Mujeres, a private school for girls. It is on Gov. Forbes, the street on the other side of the University of Santo Tomas. It has converted to co-educational to compensate for the lack of schools. Instead of repeating the fifth grade, which was interrupted last December, I take and pass a competency test that accelerates me to the sixth grade. *Ate* Nene decides to repeat the sixth grade.

Because the school is on one side of the University of Santo Tomas, and our home on the other side, to get to school, we have to go by the university, walking on the long, broad sidewalk in front of it. *Ate* Nene walks with her friends of the same age from the neighborhood. When we get to the main gate at the center, we have to stop, face the two sentries, feet together, and bow from the waist. There have been cases when people, even children, who fail to do this, are stopped or called back and slapped on both cheeks; then told to bow low. And Father has warned us of this. Most adults avoid this problem by crossing Espana Boulevard to the other side and walking on that sidewalk to get to Gov. Forbes.

I carry my books in a sort of backpack at my back with a side strap for each shoulder—the way taught us by those Philippine Scouts in Bataan—this way I have both my arms and hands free. Tommy has a small school bag hanging on his side with the strap across his body. So he also has his arms and hands free.

Tommy loves to run and skip on the broad sidewalk and I call to him sharply as we approach the center. Then I place him in front of me and hold him as I face the sentries and bow. This way Tommy gets to bow properly; I would not like to see him slapped.

One day as we bow, Tommy turns his head and looks up at me smiling and making faces. I put a hand on his face, push it down and hold it till we straighten up. I look at the sentries and see them smiling slightly, looking at each other and looking at me. I look at them puzzled, not knowing how to respond correctly. So I just bow my head and walk away, holding on to Tommy's hand. When we get home, I tell Father about it, and he says,

> You did the right thing. To the Japanese, respect is very important. Smiling back may not be considered respectful coming from a child and a subordinate because it is being familiar.

The typical school day starts at 7:30 with honoring both the Filipino and Japanese flags as they are raised in the middle of the courtyard, singing the respective national anthems. This is followed by a fifteen-minute *rajio-taiso* (Japanese calisthenics). At recess we get involved in games supervised by a physical education teacher. Ten minutes before we return to class, we go to the chapel for a recitation of the rosary.

The first twenty minutes of lunchtime is given to gardening. Each of us is assigned a small plot to be tilled and planted with different vegetables. The first day of class, we learn how to use the spade to turn over the earth, the hoe to level it out, and a small pick to dig holes for the seed or seedling. And the following days we water and weed for best results. This is hard work! Schoolchildren have never done these kinds of manual labor before. The Japanese believe that every piece of available ground be put to good use by planting edible stuff. Then while waiting for the garden to grow, we learn macramé, the technique of knotting twines of different sizes and thickness to make handbags, shopping bags, belts, and such. Again, this is the Japanese idea of producing practical things and using time efficiently and not wasting it by being idle. We are graded for these activities, so we cannot skip them.

School is let out at 3:30. When we get home, *Ate* Nene and I practice our piano lessons. Mother has made sure we continue this; our "profesora" is the older sister of one of the fifth graders.

There are several sections for the sixth grade. My section consists of very friendly children closer to my age, but I am the youngest in the class. *Ate* Nene's section consists of taller and older children. My best friends are Manuela P. (good with numbers), Lydia B. (good in grammar), Milagrosa M. (good in geography), and Charito A. (good in music). I love reading. While we eat lunch we help each other study the lessons or the assignments. The boys also have different abilities and are competitive with each other. They don't bother with the girls, except with the five of us, later, when they find out that our grades are the same as or better than theirs.

One day, during the rosary, Miguel, one of the boys in my class, who has been helping me with gardening, faints. The quick action of another boy behind him prevents him from hitting his head on the cement. The school nurse comes with a big, strong janitor who picks Miguel up and carries him to the Infirmary. After the rosary, I go to the Infirmary to see how he is doing. The nurse tells me,

> He will be okay, he is not sick. He passed out from hunger. He did not have breakfast this morning, and hardly ate supper last night. I'm having someone from the kitchen bring him a piece of bread with a scrambled egg and a cup of hot chocolate. Then I'm sending him home accompanied by the janitor.

"Will he still be here during lunchtime? I'd like to see and talk to him."

"Oh yes. I have to be sure he is strong enough to walk home."

At lunchtime I go back to the Infirmary. Miguel is still in bed sitting up eating a bowl of hot chicken soup. I ask him, "Why did you not have breakfast this morning? Didn't you like the food?"

He says, "There was not enough food. I did not want my two younger sisters to go hungry. My grandmother, who takes care of them and sometimes takes in sewing at home, has been sick for three days. So my mother who goes out every day to wash clothes or clean house for other people had to stay home to take care of all three. So, she was not able to bring home food or money and we started running out of food last night. But everything will be all right today because grandmother is better and mother went to work."

"What about your father?" I ask.

He answers, "I don't have a father. He was a soldier and was killed in Bataan. I've often told my mother that I don't have to go to school, then she doesn't have to pay for tuition. Then I can work doing things like helping out in stores or running errands for other people. But she said that my father would not like that, that he wanted me to finish and be an accountant or engineer. Then I will really earn good money and be a big help to my family." Of all the boys in the class, Miguel is the best in arithmetic.

He starts wrapping the two crusty rolls for the soup in a napkin saying, "I'm taking these home to my sisters. We seldom have bread. It is always rice. My sisters would love these."

After school, I tell my Father about Miguel. He says,

> There are many cases like his in Manila and in the provinces—widowed wives and fatherless children because of the war. It is not too bad in the provinces because of extended families and home grown food. I'm glad you talked to him. Sometimes that helps to make people feel better.

On August 2, Mother gives birth to a baby girl at the Mary Chiles Hospital. They name her Victoria after *Nanay* Toria (Mother's mother) and nickname her "Vic." She has a fair complexion and soft, wavy black hair; she is very pretty. Again, as it was in Tommy's case, because Mother is not strong enough to totally take care of her, I get to carry her around and play with her after school. When Vic is able to crawl and sit, I put her down on the hardwood floor and tell Rey to sit opposite her. Then I give Rey a ball and tell him to roll it toward Vic. Vic grabs the ball and I show her how to roll it back to Rey. They soon get the idea. Rey moves farther away, and the ball does not go straight to Vic. She swiftly crawls after it, squealing, and laughs when she gets it. Then she rolls it to Rey. They are having fun. So I watch them play as I do my homework.

How Harassment Is Used to Terrorize

Although it is peaceful, it is an uneasy kind of peace; tension and fear are still ever present because the Japanese go on midnight or early morning raids of neighborhoods looking for guerrillas that they have been informed reside or are hiding in that neighborhood. They are accompanied by a Filipino whose face is covered with a paper sack with only cut-outs for the eyes. So all the young men of the neighborhood are called out into the streets; everybody else stays indoors. Anyone the hooded man points to is pulled out by the soldiers to be taken away to Fort Santiago—a prison of unspeakable torture—and either never seen again or returned in a most horrible physical and mental state that it would have been better to have died. If the young man resists and fights, he is tackled and bayoneted. And if his family comes to his aid, they, too, are bayoneted. But sometimes the Japanese do not need any reason. They just come and choose a house at random to raid and harass or take away the household head and massacre the whole family when there is resistance.

One early morning, about 1:30 AM, our street is aroused by bright lights and a loud speaker. As I peep out our upstairs window, I see two trucks full of Japanese soldiers, armed with rifles and bayonets, who step down; one truck-load facing the houses on one side of the streets and the other, facing the houses on the opposite. Two soldiers are holding the arms of the hooded man as they lead him to the fore front. And the call for the young men begins. Father gets up, gets dressed and goes downstairs. I also get dressed and put my rubber shoes on, instead of the slippers or wooden shoes. *Ate* Nene is not around; she is on her regular visit to *Tatay* Iboy and Tiyeng. As I am going down, I hear Father unlock the front door and I see him go out into the street and close the door behind him. I run to the kitchen and get one of the kitchen knives, a small but hefty one I can handle in my left hand and I hold my double-edged switchblade knife with my right. I stand behind the window curtain, peeking out, watching as Father approaches the commander. I am remembering the knife fighting technique that *Tatay* Iboy taught *Ate* Nene and me in our forest hideout in Bataan to enable us to escape capture and rape or die fighting and taking down as many as we can. And I am ready to rush out if that Japanese commander tries to harm Father with that unsheathed sword he holds in his right hand, slashing and stabbing as many as I can—starting with the commander. The element of surprise is on my side. *Tatay* Iboy says that is always a great advantage.

Father bows to the commander who does likewise. They talk for a long while; then the commander sheaths his sword, clicks his heels and bows to Father who does the same. The commander then shouts a command and the soldiers all get on the trucks and drive away. The hooded Filipino is left behind. Father approaches him, talks to him, without unmasking him, and apparently tells him to leave. The man bows his head and shakes Father's hand and goes away. Nobody stops him. In any other neighborhood, he would have been beaten horribly and possibly killed for selling out his own people. If the Japanese have taken him with them, without any success in their search, he would have been tortured for wasting the commander's time.

As Father comes in, he sees me standing there with a knife in each hand. He carefully removes them, puts an arm around my shoulder as he leads me to sit on the sofa. He hugs me and lays his chin on my head as he softly says,

> Lita, do you know why I have you do all those exercises and let you do all those activities that make you strong physically? Why when we play softball I train you to control your feelings and be cool-headed and focused? I need you to replace me if something were to happen to me because some of the cases I have been handling are risky. I need you to take care of your mother and little brothers and sister, and not to try and save me, especially when it is an impossibility, as it was this morning; that's a whole army you would be facing. We both would surely have died. And what is to happen to your mother who is not physically strong, your three-month-old sister, one-and-a-half-year-old Rey, and four-year-old Tommy? Who would take care of them? Who would lead them to safety? Who would go for help?

I start to shake as I picture Mother who could hardly walk, carrying Vic on one arm, holding on to Rey's hand with her other hand, and Tommy holding on to Rey's other hand or clutching Mother's dress while she grieves the loss of husband and oldest child. She would not even make it halfway down the stairs. And tears flow down my cheeks. Father hugs me closer and rubs my arms and back and says,

> So here is another lesson. Faced with any situation, study it, and determine the right move to achieve the best result and the greatest good and the least harm to you. You have options in life, Lita, choose your options well. In the possibility of a fight, if you believe you cannot win, then retreat. There is no shame in that.

Mr. Congressman, our neighborhood representative to the puppet government, with many other neighborhood representatives, goes to Malacanang Palace and reports and complains about the incident to the President. He reports back to our neighborhood association leaders that the Japanese High Command promises to put a stop to these raiding incidents when the President persuades him that it is the wrong move in trying to win the trust of the people and prevent a general uprising. Such neighborhood raids in Manila diminish and finally stop.

The incursions, invasions, and defilement of homes are worst in the provinces. There, villages are invaded; livestock, other food, and supplies forcibly taken away; the young, old, and sick are beaten or killed when they resist; the women, young and old, are raped. Father hears from a cousin visiting us, that in Pampanga, where they are from, after such a raid in one village, the Japanese garrison finds ten dead Japanese soldiers at their gate the next morning. A big note, pinned on one of the dead says,

> For every man, woman, child, you harm, we will kill two of yours. We know who you are and where you are, but you don't know who we are and where we are.

The following raid is more ferocious, and the retaliation is as fierce and immediate, as a whole convoy of Japanese soldiers are found dead; on the highway, all their ammunition and truck batteries removed. The note this time says, "we will be taking five instead of two."

One day a whole village is set on fire because there are no villagers or livestock or supplies; the village has been forewarned and evacuated. The next morning, the dead raiders, including the officers in command, are outside the garrison's gate, again deprived of their ammunition. The raids start decreasing as raiding parties are no longer sent out because the raiders do not come back alive or never return at all, and the avengers are back in the jungles. The news spreads rapidly to all the provinces and some start to take the same action. After a short while, all the raids stop. The Japanese try a new tactic of trying to live with the people.

How Collaborators Instill Fear

Everyone knows that the attacks against the Japanese are made by the guerrillas that have formed in the different provinces when the Japanese invaded and started their atrocities against the citizens. At the start, they are just small bunches of men—fathers, husbands, grandfathers, brothers, sons—armed only with knives, *bolos* (long, big heavy knives), hatchets, bow and arrows, and spears made of sharpened bamboo poles, without a true leader, and not very organized. No one has military training. But they are fearless, good at sneak attacks and ambush, especially in the forests and jungles. Their sole purpose is to defend home and family.

Then when they are joined by those American soldiers and Philippine Scouts who escaped the Death March and those who survived it after being rescued and cared for by townspeople, the guerrilla movements begin to be organized, and their purpose changes from defense to attack. Their attacks on the Japanese show military precision and discipline and applications of military tactics and strategies. They start arming themselves by capturing all the guns and ammunition of the Japanese that they attack. They are practically invisible; they live in the jungles and hills or merge subtly with the people in the towns and villages; some are said to be inside the Japanese camps.

Then when the Philippine Military Academy (PMA) in Baguio—a military academy patterned after the U.S. West Point Academy—is closed down, some of the PMA officers and cadets start, or join, guerrilla units. Later a group of young ROTC cadets from the different universities in Manila join in, taking their practice rifles with them, but not many bullets. But these cadets have been military trained and disciplined and are skilled fighters in hand to hand combat with knives or in "Arnis" (a Philippine martial art of self-defense using one or two short but solid wooden sticks or canes). So they not only add to the growing military fighting units, but they also help train more young recruits. The Japanese ban ROTC in the curriculum of all the colleges and universities.

Dolfo, the second son of our resident from Nueva Ecija (who donates rice to our co-op), is one of these ROTC cadets and is now a high-ranking guerrilla officer in Nueva Ecija. He comes to visit his family often, but not on a regular basis. His sister, Mely, who is about my age, is my best friend, and we go to each others house to play or chat. Their residence, like ours, is third from us in a series of six connected townhouses. I often see Dolfo when he comes and he always ruffles my hair when he sees me.

During his visits, Dolfo tells us what is happening in the provinces. One day when we (my family, the families of some of the neighborhood association officers, and Father's chess mates) are having lunch at his family's house on one of his visits, he starts giving us news about the the progress of the war, from the "underground." When I ask Father what is the *underground*, he says,

> it is an espionage unit, purely military, unlike the guerrilla movement which deals with the Japanese on the civilian level. It spies on the Japanese and their military strength, movements and plans, and relays the information to the Allies (the Americans, the British, the Australians, and all those who side with them in fighting against Germany and Japan). It also relays, to the guerrillas, news of the Allies' activities regarding the Philippines to alert and make them ready for the liberation.

"And what is *liberation*?"

"It is the time when the Americans will take over the country from the Japanese and return us to democracy and the life we used to have before the war. But you don't have to worry or think or talk about this. This is a consideration for the adults."

Dolfo says, "that is right. It can also be very dangerous to discuss this in public because there might be a *makapili* around. These are Filipinos, so you cannot know or distinguish them, or set them apart. They are Japanese collaborators who spy for the Japanese for money or other benefits. That hooded Filipino with the Japanese who raided our neighborhood, is a *makapili.* How he knew or suspected the presence of a guerrilla in the neighborhood, we will never know. We, the guerrillas, do have ways of finding out and punishing, if harm is done. Since no harm was done at that time, thanks to our neighborhood association's president, Atty. Yumol, we let it go. If the *makapilis* hear anyone say anything against the Japanese or talk about the Americans or liberation, or guerrillas, they will call the Japanese and point out the person who will be picked up and brought to Fort Santiago. If they hear it from children, then they will accuse the fathers saying that the children must have heard it at home. So, Lita, Mely, do not discuss or talk about, or even mention, these anywhere or with anyone. Even if someone in a gathering you're in says something on this subject, don't agree, or offer any ideas; just ignore and look for an excuse to move away. You don't know (1) if a *makapili* is around or (2) the more likely possibility, that the speaker may be a *makapili* deceptively trying to encourage people to speak and vent their feelings. Promise, or your fathers will suffer."

Mely and I nod our heads and say, "yes, we promise." And we go back to playing Chinese checkers.

Then someone says, "it is really ironic and sad that we start distrusting our own people; that we fear our compatriots more than we fear the Japanese."

Christmas this year, 1942, is gloomy and sad. Because of curfew, the traditional colorful and creative paper and bamboo lanterns are not hung on the windows to light the way for the door-to-door carolers. The streets are dark, silent; the midnight mass is canceled. There are no gifts for the children, and in some neighborhoods some homes don't have enough food. Cooked rice is expanded by mixing it with sweet potato, and chicken soup is filled with lots of vegetables to fill up on and not notice how very few are the pieces of chicken meat.

How a Personal Triumph Awakens Hope

One day our Nipongo teacher, Miss P., who has just arrived from a year at the University of Tokyo, asks the class, "Who has experience going up on a stage and declaiming?"

No one raises a hand, so I raise my hand and say, "I have been declaiming since Grade Three at the Sta. Isabel College, ma'am."

She says, "Good! I will give your name and will recommend you to the school committee that will select the school's representative to the National Elocution Contest at the Metropolitan Theater." This theater is a popular cultural and art center presenting musical concerts, art shows of paintings or sculptures, folk dances, elocution contests, and drama. It is big and beautiful with wood carvings of Philippine animals and flowers. Sometime it is used to show movies when there are no cultural activities.

The next day she says to me, "Isabel, during recess, go to the gymnasium."

Once there, I see four boys and two other girls. Each one of us is asked to go on stage and read two long paragraphs in Japanese.

The following day, Miss P. announces to the class, "the committee has chosen Isabel. She is the best reader and has an authentic Japanese pronunciation." My classmates clap and cheer. She says to me, "Isabel, I will choose the piece, you will read it to me and memorize it. Then I will coach you for emotive delivery and gesture every day during recess. We have two weeks to prepare."

When I get home and tell my parents, *Tatay* Iboy, and Tiyeng who are visiting, both smilingly say, "And did your teacher also say that you look like a Japanese girl, like your good friends, the Tanaka girls who used to be your neighbors? Whatever happened to them?"

"Ah, yes," I tell them, "I remember the Tanaka family who lived on our street before the War. I used to go to their house on some weekends and play with their two daughters, Mari and Suri, my age. Mrs. Tanaka was a kind woman, always smiling when Mr. Tanaka was not at home. She always wore the Japanese kimono and the Japanese wooden shoes that separate the big toe from the rest. She served us some Japanese hot tea and crackers and rice cakes, and she talked to me in Japanese. I did not understand most of what she said, but she made sure I learned some courtesy words like *arigato gozaimasu* (thank you, very much), *sayonara* (good bye), *ohayo gozaimasu* (good morning), *konichiwa* (good afternoon), *kombawa* (good evening), and *tomodachi* (friend). Mr. Tanaka, who owned a bazaar in Quiapo (one of the business centers in Manila), was always serious, never smiled, and ignored us. When he was home, we had to play in the patio and told not to be noisy. I went home whenever he got home."

Mr. Villa tells us that the Tanakas left when evacuation was ordered. Some people say that they went back to Japan. Mr. Tanaka's bazaar is now a "bombay" store run by a tall "bombay" who has a beard and wears a turban.

Miss P. is a very diligent coach. I ask her one time to translate and explain the piece that I have memorized, believing I can declaim better knowing what I am saying. She says,

> No. Your pronunciation is very good but I want you to emote and deliver like a Japanese girl, that Japanese girl in the story. If you understand it, then you might see the scene and events as Filipino and you will react to them as a Filipino and miss the essence. I want you to be Japanese; so just follow my coaching. When you are on that stage, you are that Japanese girl.

So Father, who has been coaching me in my previous declamations, cannot help. But he thinks Miss P. is correct.

On the day of the elocution, there are four girls and six boys. I am the youngest and the smallest and the only one from the grade school. We sit in the back of the stage facing the audience. The theater is full. My parents, Tommy, *Ate* Nene, and my uncles, *Tyo* Nonong and *Tyo* Tenyong (Father's brothers), *Tya* Ines (*Tyo* Nonong's wife), and *Tya* Anchang (Father's sister) are there, as well as some friends of Father. *Tatay* Iboy and Tiyeng are at home looking after Rey and Vic. In the first row of seats, right in front of the stage, sit three Japanese generals and behind them, their aides. And the declamations begin.

When it is my turn, I walk to the front of the stage, stand straight, look at the generals and bow low; I am the only one of the contestants to do this (Miss P. advised me to do this before I took my seat on stage when she saw the generals). Many times during my delivery, the generals show some slight reactions. My piece ends with me looking upward to the sky, with upraised hands, left slightly higher than the right, pleading, then fall down on my knees and sit on my heels with head bowed, my hands clasped on my lap. The theater is in a loud roar of applause. I raise my head, surprised. And as I stand up, I see the three generals on their feet and applauding, their clapping hands raised toward me. The crowd's elation and joy, at seeing the generals on their feet and applauding, are so palpable, raising the hope that someday we may be respected and treated kindly. I bow low before going back to my seat.

A short intermission of Japanese music and dance follows the last contestant. Then the head of the judging committee gets up on stage and say, "We have decided on three prizes: first prize, gold medal; second prize, silver medal; and third prize, bronze medal. As your name is called come forward to receive your medal."

He calls the name of the first prize winner, a first year high school boy from the Ateneo de Manila High School (a Jesuit school for boys), who comes forward and faces the award presenter, gets his medal, then goes back to his seat. Applause. The man continues, "Second prize, silver medal, Isabel Yumol, sixth grader, Instituto de Mujeres." Applause. I walk to the front of the stage, face the award presenter and bow my head as he puts the ribbon over my head and down to my neck. Then I turn to face the audience and bow to the generals who nod their heads. I walk back to my seat. The third prize winner is a second year high school boy from Mapa High School (public school). Again I am the only one to bow before the generals.

Everyone in our group is happy, kissing and hugging me, especially my parents. My parents take me, our relatives and friends, and Miss P. to a restaurant.

One of Father's friends says, "I am surprised that the Japanese, high-ranking ones too, were there. And they showed appreciation."

Father says, "It is not really surprising because first, I'm sure they were invited, and second, this must be one of their new ways of trying to earn the trust of the people."

Someone comments, "you know, our little personal triumphs, like this, permitted and appreciated, make us feel less oppressed and subjugated."

After school ends on March 31, 1943, and I pass sixth grade, my parents enroll me at Sta. Rita College High School. Tommy is also enrolled there, but *Ate* Nene does not like nuns, and so she is enrolled at the Legarda High School, a public high school. In June, a month after my eleventh birthday, I start first-year high school. Tommy, who celebrated his fifth birthday in April, is in the Kindergarten.

Sta. Rita College is far from our neighborhood, unlike the Instituto de Mujeres which is just on the other side of the University of Sto. Tomas and is reached by a direct route across the University sidewalk on Espana. Sta. Rita can be reached in two ways. One way is from our street Cataluna cross Espana Boulevard (a major street, wide and divided by a median) on to where Cataluna ends on Lepanto (a main street); right on Lepanto to where it ends on Azcarraga (a main street), cross Azcarraga and turn left to where it ends on Legarda (a main street); turn right. Sta. Rita's front courtyard and portal of double doors are on Legarda.

The other way is to turn left on Gastambide (a residential street where Mary Chiles Hospital is located) from Lepanto to Legarda, cross Azcarraga on Legarda to Sta. Rita's front courtyard. Although this school is far and the way circuitous, we still have to walk because there is no available transportation. But it is possible to walk it because it is not across the Pasig River. Tommy and I walk to Sta. Rita College every day, from Monday to Friday, taking the Gastambide route because it is more scenic; the houses have small front yards with trees and flowers.

We leave the house at about 7:15 in the morning for the start of classes at 8:00. This way we don't have to run or hurry, and we arrive at school calm and fresh. When my classes end at 4:00, Tommy, whose classes end at 3:30, waits for me in the garden with some of his friends or in a chair by the piano in the lobby whose double front doors are closed and locked. A nun (*portera*) sits at a desk next to them.

How a Personal Tragedy Numbs National Loss

Sometime in mid-March 1944, Vic wakes up whimpering; she hardly cries, even when she falls down as she toddles around. Mother picks her up and says that she is burning with fever. Dr. Prospero is out of town on vacation. One of the doctors residing on our street comes over and prescribes a fourth of Cafiaspirina to lessen the fever and lots of water. That seems to help. But that evening, Vic starts crying and crying, moving her head from side to side. By this time Mother is exhausted from carrying Vic around; I take Vic from her and lay her head on my shoulder to stop the movement and kiss her forehead and gently rub her head. She seems to like that and she falls asleep. Then in the middle of the night, she wakes up and cries loudly and incessantly, not just sobbing. Father gets up, picks her up, walks around the room, and sings to her, and she falls asleep. But when Father puts her down, she wakes up and starts the crying again. So when she falls asleep after Father picks her up and walks around with her, he sits on the rocking chair, his hand supporting and gently patting her back. At about mid-morning, the next day, she wakes up screaming as if in pain. Both Father and Mother take turns trying to calm her to no avail. They try wetting her lips with cool water; the screams subside to be replaced by crying. At a point when she screams, she also clutches tightly at anything within reach—Father's ear. Mother's hair, my fingers, as if grasping for help. The poor baby looks exhausted and weakening.

So they call a priest to give emergency baptism. It is customary in our country to wait for a special occasion to have children baptized. This time, they feel, it can't wait. Vic is screaming and grabbing and kicking as Mother and Father hold her and offer her head to the priest for the Holy Water. The priest goes through the ritual slowly pouring the water on Vic's forehead. As the water slowly runs down her whole head, Vic's screams, cries, and struggles subside and she becomes calm. But after a long while she starts up again.

Tatay Iboy, who has come with Tiyeng to help out, says, "the water seems to have an effect. It probably cools her burning fever. So why don't you put an ice-pack on her head."

That helps a lot. Vic is calmer; she no longer screams or cries, but she moans and sometimes heaves a deep sigh; her eyes close as Father cradles her in his arms. At around 4:00 in the afternoon, my parents decide to take her to the hospital.

Father is recovering from a malaria attack, so Mother bundles Vic up and tells *Ate* Nene to hail down a *calesa.* Although Mary Chiles, on Gastambide, is not very far (Sta. Rita is even farther, past Mary Chiles), going by *calesa* will be faster and less stressful than walking. But the problem is that it is hard to get one, so *Ate* Nene runs to Espana to find one. Mother does not want to wait, so she goes out and starts walking fast.

Father tells me, "Lita go with your Mother."

I grab the ice bag and catch up with Mother and hold the ice bag on Vic's head as I match stride with Mother. And I am thinking that if it were not for this war, *Tatay* Iboy would still have his car and have Berto drive us to the hospital, or there would be lots of taxicabs, or even an ambulance that the hospital would send. And I look up at Mother, brave, fiercely determined—even in her physically frail condition—to bring her daughter to the hospital for help. And she has always been like this to each of us—self-sacrificing, personally attentive, and caring.

We meet up with *Ate* Nene almost at the corner of Espana. When we get on the *calesa, Ate* Nene sits on one side of Mother by Vic's head, holding the ice pack. I sit on the other side of Mother and see the driver make a wrong turn and misses Gastambide. I tell him and so he has to turn around and retrace. At the emergency room of the hospital, after examining Vic and learning of her condition, the doctor decides to give her an intravenous injection. The doctor cannot find a good vein in either arm to put in the solution. So he decides to use the bigger vein in the leg, finds it and injects the solution, but it spews out; the vein has closed. Vic heaves a deep sigh, opens her eyes and looks at us, then closes them and breathes her last.

Mother, who is sitting on a chair by the bed, holding Vic's hand and caressing her arm, lays her head down close to Vic's, puts an arm around her little body, and weeps deeply but quietly. I stand helpless, unable to do anything, nor even knowing what I can do. And I feel so inadequate. . . . We have been through so much hardship and suffering, been through all kinds of deprivation and physical discomfort, but we have fought back and survived. But this . . . what does one do with emotional pain? I see the day calendar on the wall; it is March 17, 1944. Vic is only one year, seven months, and fifteen days old.

The doctor turns to me and says, "Lita go home and tell your father to come over. We need him here." Ate Nene decides to stay with Mother. Although she is only fifteen, she has been most helpful and emotionally steady all throughout the ordeal; she has been taking on lots of responsibilities. She seems to have grown up quickly.

As I walk through the lobby on my way out, the wall clock chimes 6:30 o'clock. I run all the way home, tears rolling down my cheeks, already feeling Vic's absence. When Father opens the door and sees me, he drops to one knee and enfolds me in a hug as he rubs my back as I keep sobbing.

After a while I tell him, "*Tay* (Dad), the doctor wants you at the hospital. *Nanay* (Mom) needs you."

He stands up, after wiping my tears, and says, "Lita, let's say a prayer and thank God for ending Vic's suffering. She is now cured and happy in heaven with God and she wants us to be happy too. She will be watching over us from above."

The funeral mass is beautiful; so many people and fragrant flowers, beautiful music, and figures of cherubs. The priest talks about Vic, God's little angel sent to us to give us beauty, peace, and joy, if only for a while, to make us forget what we have been through. And now her work is finished and she is called back to heaven. All throughout the ceremony, Father has an arm around Mother's shoulders, which are trembling with silent sobs, his eyes somber, sad, and red. After the ceremony, a white dove is set free; it circles around us, then flies up to the high ceiling and disappears. The personal sorrow and deep sense of loss shared by all those around us seem to diminish the national sadness and tragedy of losing our country and being subjugated.

When Dr. Prospero arrives from his vacation, he calls to check on us. Mother tells him about Vic and how nobody seemed to know what the problem was. He comes over, gives Mother her regular injection for her rheumatism, and after listening, he says, "Vic's symptoms show she contracted meningitis; this is almost always fatal, especially in children. It is an infection in the brain, causing inflammation. That is why she found relief with the water and the ice pack. They cooled the burning fever in her brain."

Dr. Prospero is a religious man, a devout Catholic, so he talks about Vic, the way the priest did at the funeral. He says, "Vic is an angel sent to be with Rey. She was a great help in Rey's healing; always there next to him, playing with him, cheering him up, making him laugh and keeping him from feeling bad when he was sick. She left when he has recovered fully; her work was finished. Now Rey feels Vic's absence. He no longer needs medical supervision. He needs a special kind of care and attention."

Time heals wounds and eases pain. When Mother enrolls Tommy and me at Sta. Rita College in June 1944, for my second year in high school and Tommy's first grade, she takes three-year-old Rey with her. Then she takes us to a refreshment parlor and treats us to a glass each of *halo-halo*, a Filipino cold dessert made of a mixture of fruits and a variety of beans in coconut milk and sugar, topped with shaved ice. Rey is delighted.

Often Tommy and I go home by ourselves. But sometimes Mother, with Rey, comes to pick us up after some shopping at Quiapo, the busiest shopping center in the heart of Manila. It is also the location of the Quiapo Church and its famous statue of the Black Nazarene, a life-size dark wood sculpture of Jesus carrying the cross. The nun at the lobby lets Mother in and she waits in the lobby. Rey enjoys these trips and runs to us when he sees us.

How U.S. Planes in the Sky Signal Liberation

One evening at the end of one of our co-op fund-raising events, when the Japanese officer and his men and other neighborhood association guests have left, and while our women residents are cleaning up and clearing everything away, our men sit at one table, smoking, drinking coffee, and chatting. Mr. Villa says, "According to my short-wave radio, the American forces have begun air strikes in the Marianas Islands of Saipan and Guam. If they are successful, then they would be coming toward the Philippines."

Dolfo adds, "that is true. We received the news from the underground. The air strikes are successful and they are getting ready for the amphibious landing and assault. We are next."

Someone asks, "Where will they strike first—Mindanao, Visayas, or Luzon?"

Dolfo says, "hard to say. Only one thing comes out clear—get to Manila as fast as possible to liberate the concentration and internment camps before the Japanese kill the prisoners. So you in your neighborhood need to be alert because you are so close to the University of Santo Tomas and the Bilibid Prison. I will let you know. I don't want you to start any activity that will arouse the suspicions of the *makapili* and the Japanese. Go on with your lives as usual. You did not hear any of these."

At the Sta. Rita College, all the high school classes are on the second floor; the grade school classes on the first or ground floor. One of my classes in the second year is biology. Our laboratory is on the corner of the building giving it two walls with a window on each wall, one facing the front and the other facing the side. These windows are tall and wide, almost the length of the walls. They are open and have unobstructed view of the outside. A long table along these windows hold the microscopes for better lighting. The microscope assigned to me is on the table facing front looking out into the front courtyard and at the Legarda/Tanduay Streets.

One morning as we are busy with the microscopes, I hear a drone like the sound of many airplanes. We have become used to the sound of one or two Japanese airplanes that fly the skies now and then. But this sound is steady and growing louder. I look up from the microscope and see at the distant horizon on Tanduay Street a whole dark moving shape, moving fast. As it gets closer, I see several airplanes in some kind of formation, dark without the big and round red rising sun symbol.

I shout, "American airplanes!" I push aside the microscopes in front of me and scramble onto the table, look out the window in time to see two-bodied airplanes passing by overhead. I shout my wonder and excitement. And my classmates rush to the windows, too, trying to look out across the table. Then the air-raid sirens start to blare out loudly and I see small white puffs of smoke in the sky. The two bodied airplanes move so fast none of the white puffs is hitting them. And I hear the answering rat-a-tat of machine gun fire coming from the two-bodied airplanes as they swiftly dive. The nuns start ordering everybody to go downstairs. I crane my neck out the window, looking to my right, and see the Japanese airplanes coming from afar and approaching the American airplanes. A group of the two-bodied American airplanes separate to meet the Japanese airplanes. Two nuns come to pull me away from the window. I snatch my backpack, glance at the wall day calendar (it shows September 21, 1944), and run downstairs to get Tommy.

The garden is full of people, running, moving fast in every direction, talking loudly and at the same time; some are crying. It is chaotic. I enter the lobby; this, too, is full of people, but quieter. I cannot see Tommy because it is crowded. I know he is here, in the chair by the piano. I have often told him that he should stay there in case of any emergency until I get to him, rather than look for me. I make my way through the thick crowd toward the piano as I call out his name. And I hear "*ate*" from the direction of the piano and I see his shoulder and head above the crowd because he is standing tip-toe on the piano bench. I go to him and stand by him waiting for any instruction. Some of the parents, who live nearby, come to take their children home, and as they leave the crowd thins a bit.

A nun rings a bell to get attention. She says, "We ask everybody to go home, except for the young ones in grade school who should wait until their parents come to get them, as they have always done."

That, of course, exempts Tommy because he always goes home with me. And since I have to go home now, as instructed, then he has to come home with me. So I tell Tommy, "We will be going home now. We will be careful. We may have to run most of the way so we can get home sooner and out of danger. Do you understand? And you must do what I tell you to, okay?" Tommy nods.

The all-clear signal has not sounded, so there must still be some fighting going on. When we get to the front door, I look out, all around, and up at the sky. It is clear; I don't see any airplanes. I decide to take Azcarraga instead of Gastambide because there will be more people there, very tall townhouses and some stores and offices. So Tommy and I cross the courtyard fast. Turn left on Legarda and left again on Azcarraga. There are many people out, running, walking fast, coming and going in every direction.

The townhouses on Azcarraga are different from ours in that they are taller because they are two-family townhouses: one family lives on the first floor which has a mezzanine for the bedrooms thus adding height to the building; another family lives upstairs on one floor. To get to the second-floor residence, a long staircase leads up from the street. This staircase is shared with another residence across from it, which also has its own downstairs residence. Thus, the staircase is in the middle of these two buildings and is enclosed on either side by their external walls. Because of this set-up, there is no street door in front at the bottom of the staircase. The doors to the two second-floor residences are opposite each other on the upstairs landing. I noted this difference from our townhouse a long time ago when one of my classmates in fourth grade at the Sta. Isabel, who lived in one of upper residences, had a birthday party.

About midway on Azcarraga, walking fast on the sidewalk in front of the townhouses, we hear the distant drone of airplanes getting louder and coming in our direction. Then the popping and rat-a-tat sounds start up. We need to get out of the wide open area and so I tell Tommy to run to the nearest stairwell. I push him into the stairwell and I follow. We climb to about half-way up the staircase and sit down. It is a perfect air-raid shelter! When it seems quieter, I go down, look out, and see people going about on the street. I call to Tommy and we cross to the other side. Just as we reach the corner with Lepanto, we hear a loud explosion behind us. I push Tommy to the stairwell of the last set of townhouses at the corner and follow him. This time a lot of people follow us in and we are pushed higher up. I feel more secure with all those adults in front of us. Lots of people are running outside. A group of strong-looking young men with buckets and a hydrant hose pass by saying that the explosion started a fire. They will help put out the fire to stop it from spreading to the nearby homes. The adults in front of us start leaving. And we follow.

Before turning right on Lepanto toward Cataluna, I hesitate because it is a long way and there are no townhouses with their sheltering staircases. We really have to make a run for it. Then I remember the refreshment parlor on Lepanto where Mother takes us for *halo-halo*, and a neighborhood store on the corner of Cataluna and Espana. I am hoping they are open and we could find shelter in them if needed. If not, I will have to knock on somebody's house and ask to be let in. I tell Tommy all these. Then we start on the run. I hold Tommy's hand as I keep pace with him. He is doing very well.

A young couple, who has been attending our neighborhood fund drives, and who lives on P. Noval this side of Espana, catches up with us and says, "Lita, we will stay with you to the corner of Espana and Cataluna instead of going straight on Lepanto to P. Noval right now."

There is a lot of activity and rumbling in the sky but not close to us. At the corner, I thank the young couple who says, "We will wait to see you cross Espana safely before we turn right."

When the traffic eases up, Tommy and I make a dash across the wide Espana. We are nearly home. Then the all-clear signal sounds. We slow down to a walk.

Mother is surprised to see us alone but very relieved. She says, "Your Father was supposed to come for you from his office. Why did you leave and come home on your own?"

I answer, "because the nuns told us to; they were ordering everybody out except for the young grade school children whose parent or guardian always comes to take them home."

Ate Nene, with some of her neighborhood friends, arrives a little after us. A bit later Father arrives home and sees us safe. He pats my back and Tommy's head. Mother tells him what I told her.

He says, "that's right. That's what I was told when I got there looking for Lita and Tommy. I spoke to the Mother Directress and told her that their decision to let the students go home, during an air-raid situation, was wrong and put the students in harm's way. She said that they only let the high school students, who were at least fourteen years old and knew enough to take care of themselves, go home. They kept the children until their parents arrived. I told her that she was making two false assumptions: first, not all high school students are fourteen years old; that my daughter, although she is in the second year, is only twelve. And she would be taking care of her brother who is only six. Second, not all those who have reached fourteen know enough to take care of themselves in an emergency situation, if they have never been in one."

At supper, I excitedly tell everyone about the fast-moving two-bodied American airplanes. Father says, "the American liberation of the Philippines from the Japanese has begun. We have to start stocking up for an emergency again like in 1941."

Mother says, "That's fine. But I will not evacuate; I will not leave this house."

Father responds, "no, of course not. The events are different. In fact, if what Dolfo said is correct, Manila will be liberated first and immediately made secure. So we should be safer here than anywhere."

And so we begin again filling up all kinds of containers with water, buying and storing large amounts of staples—rice, yams, salt and sugar, canned food—matches, batteries, flashlights, firewood, medicines, etc.

And I find myself thinking, "I've been here before, except that I was nine then and now I'm twelve."

Photos and Maps

Mother

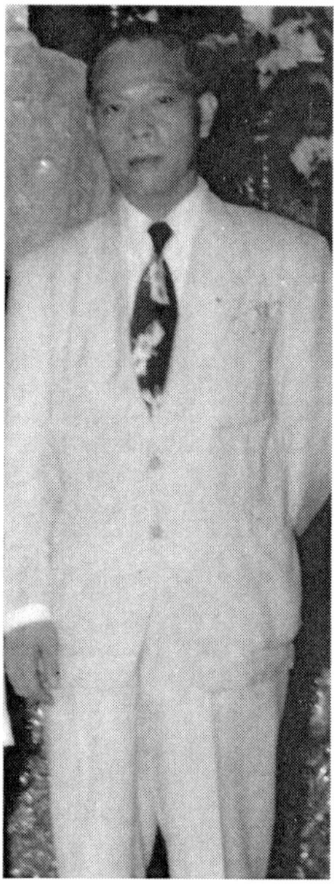

Father

Lita, nine years old

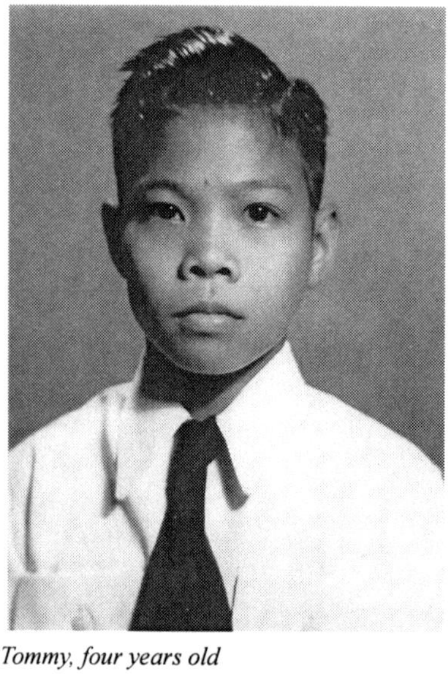

Tommy, four years old

Milkmaid condensed milk

Kilm powdered milk

Facade of Santa Isabel College, Intramuros

A rice field in Bataan

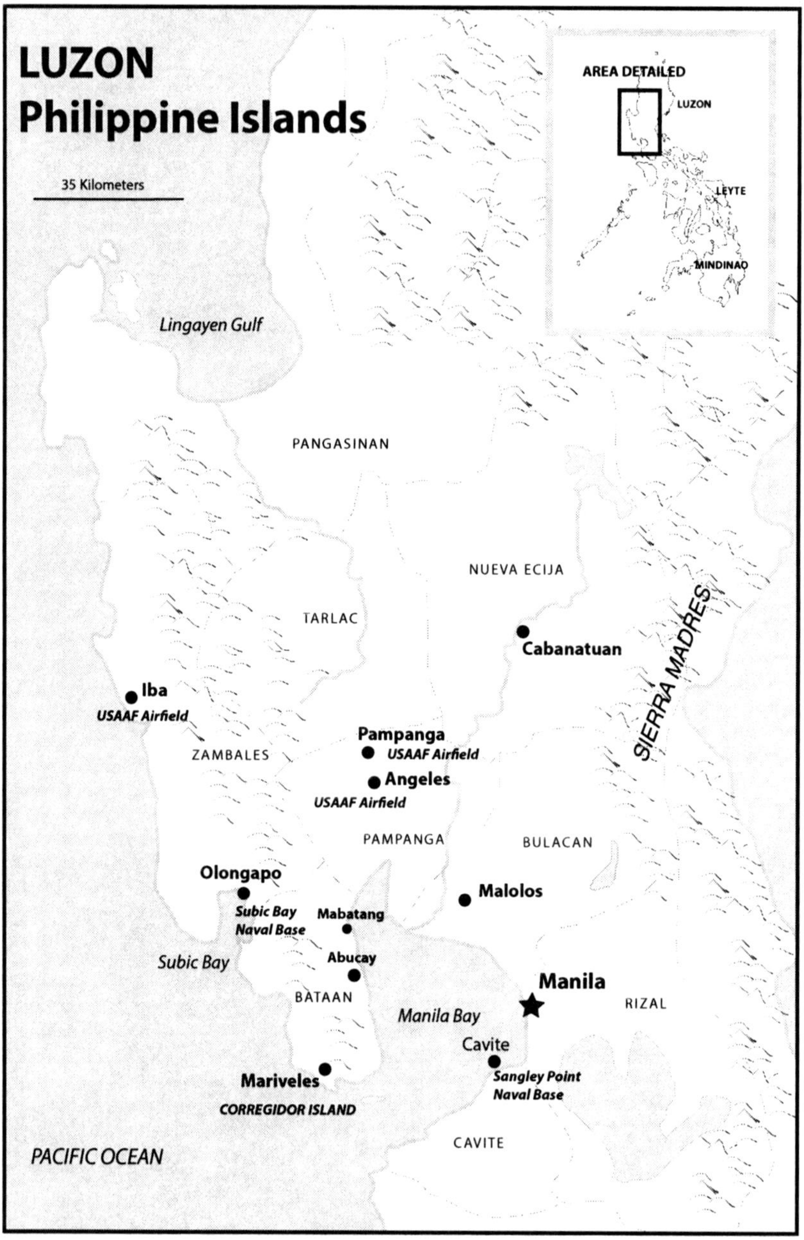
LUZON
Philippine Islands
35 Kilometers
AREA DETAILED
LUZON
LEYTE
MINDINAO
Lingayen Gulf
PANGASINAN
NUEVA ECIJA
TARLAC
Cabanatuan
SIERRA MADRES
Iba
USAAF Airfield
Pampanga
USAAF Airfield
ZAMBALES
Angeles
USAAF Airfield
PAMPANGA
BULACAN
Olongapo
Malolos
Subic Bay
Naval Base
Mabatang
Subic Bay
Abucay
Manila
BATAAN
Manila Bay
RIZAL
Cavite
Mariveles
Sangley Point
Naval Base
CORREGIDOR ISLAND
CAVITE
PACIFIC OCEAN

Philippine woven sleeping mat (banig)

Weaving of banig

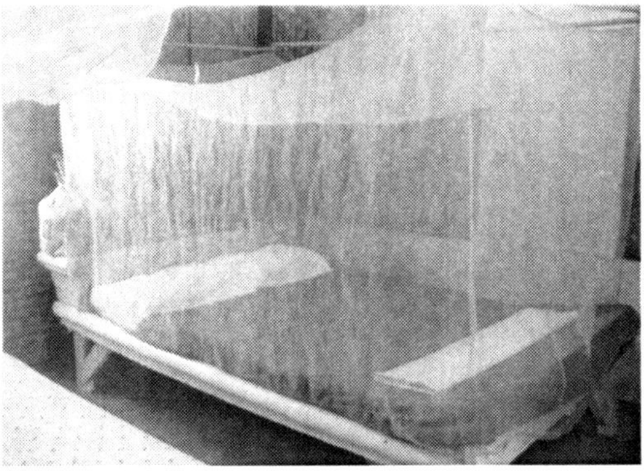

A mosquito net (kulambo)

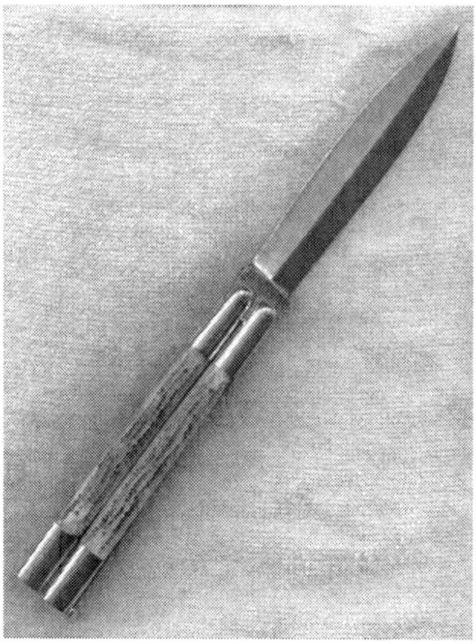

Balisong, double-edged switchblade knife

Punyal, double-edged combat knife

Rice paddies filled with water ready for planting

Carretela, a form of public transportation

Calesa, a form of public transportation

Calesas in traffic (traffic police under umbrella).

University of Santo Tomas, front view facing Espana Blvd.

University of Santa Tomas, wrought iron wall next to front gate on Espana Blvd., showing notice that it is an internment camp

Patinetro, Filipino's children's game (three players as guards standing on the the line, and three players trying to cross the line)

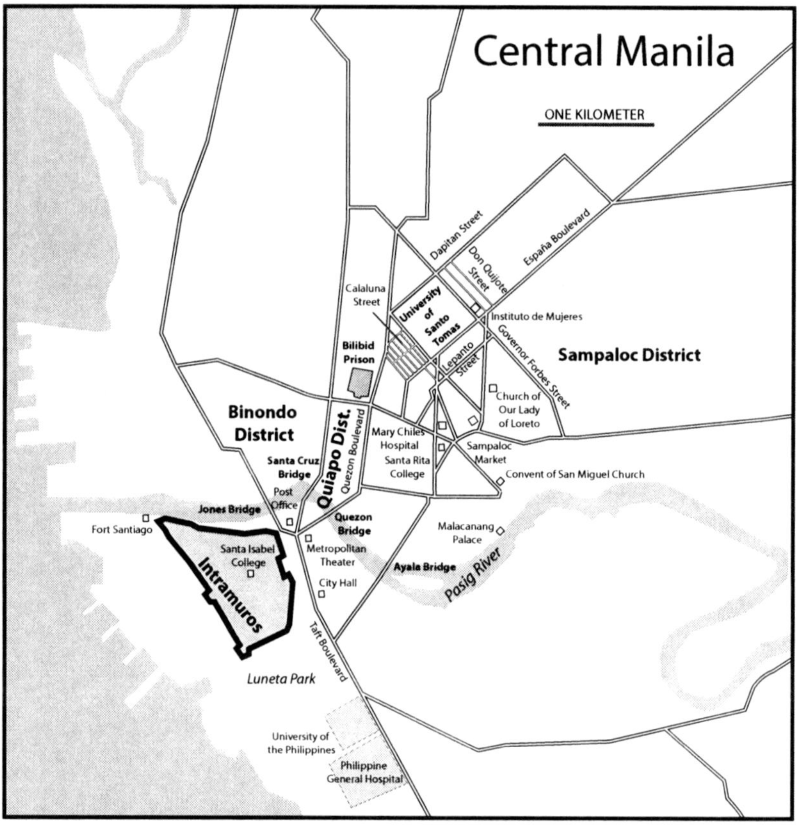
Central Manila
ONE KILOMETER
Dapitan Street
España Boulevard
Don Quijote Street
Calaluna Street
University of Santo Tomas
Instituto de Mujeres
Governor Forbes Street
Sampaloc District
Bilibid Prison
Lepanto Street
Church of Our Lady of Loreto
Binondo District
Quiapo Dist.
Quezon Boulevard
Mary Chiles Hospital
Santa Rita College
Sampaloc Market
Santa Cruz Bridge
Convent of San Miguel Church
Post Office
Jones Bridge
Quezon Bridge
Fort Santiago
Malacanang Palace
Santa Isabel College
Metropolitan Theater
Intramuros
Ayala Bridge
City Hall
Pasig River
Taft Boulevard
Luneta Park
University of the Philippines
Philippine General Hospital

Pasig River

Philippine Flag

Japanese Flag

Rajio-taiso *performed by schoolchildren*

Schoolchildren gardening

Macramé knots

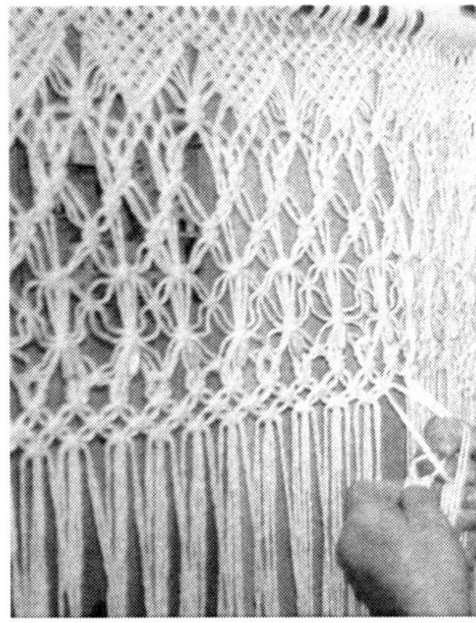

Finished macramé piece

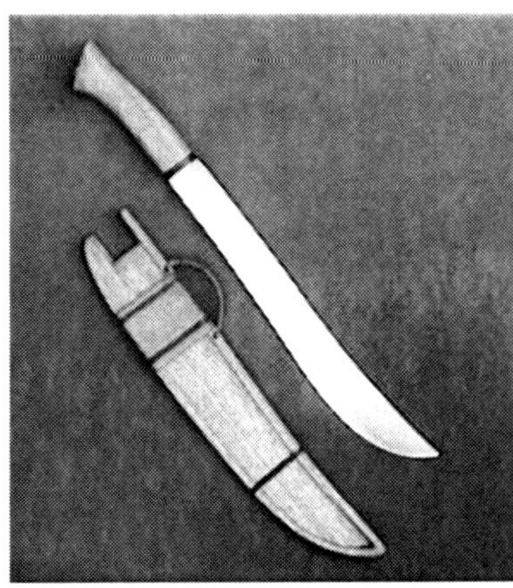

Filipino bolo

Arnis, hand-to-hand combat using sturdy sticks.

Parol, Filipino Christmas lanterns made of bamboo and colored paper lit by a small bulb.

Metropolitan Theater

Ate Nene and me; she is fifteen and I am twelve.

Halo-halo, *refreshment made of mixed fruit, red beans, coconut milk, and crushed ice.*

Statue of the Black Nazarene at the front altar of the Quiapo Church.

U.S. P-38 two-bodied airplanes in the Philippine sky, September 21, 1944.

Quiapo Church, facade

Sari-sari, *family-owned neighborhood store.*

Malacanang Palace, Philippine president's office and residence.

Ruins of our neighborhood after the conflagration from Japanese incendiary bombing; tower of Sto. Thomas University seen on upper left.

The "little American flag" children waved to greet the American liberators.

Small can of "Nescafe," part of food package distributed by the American liberators.

"Jeepneys," U.S. military jeeps converted to public transportation.

Father and Rey, 1944. Rey is three years old.

Tommy, Rey, and me, 1946. Tommy is eight years old. Rey is five, and I am fourteen.

Mother and Tommy, 1945. Tommy is seven years old.

Ate Nene and me, 1946. Ate Nene is seventeen years old and I am fourteen years old.

Isabel College uniform, 1946.

Philippine Independence Ceremony, raising the Philippine Flag, Luneta Park, Manila.

American Liberation of Manila: September 21, 1944–July 4, 1946

Battling for Control of the Philippine Sea

Again classes are suspended and schools are closed. Again total blackout and curfew are ordered. And so the black heavy curtains come out and are hung on all the windows.

One day Mr. S., Dolfo's father, calls Father and asks him over, and adds, "bring Lita with you."

Mr. Villa and some of the officers of the neighborhood association are also there. When I see Dolfo, I tell him about the two-bodied American airplanes. I say, "They are fast moving and the white puffs did not hit them. But they did not drop any bombs."

Dolfo says, "they are not bombers. They are fighter planes to engage the Japanese planes into a dog-fight. Those white puffs are from anti-aircraft guns meant to bring them down. So they dive and strafe them to get them out."

Then he turns to everyone and says, "you know that the battle of the Philippine sea began in June. They have been successful in that. That is why the American airplanes started showing up. They are now hitting Mindanao. Soon General MacArthur will be landing. You can now start stocking up for an emergency. It will not seem unusual because the curfew, blackouts, and air-raid alarms are signs of an emergency."

A lot of questions and discussion follow. I tell Mely, "my Father started us on that emergency preparations after I told him about the two-bodied American airplanes. How about your family?"

Mely doesn't say anything; she is unusually quiet. Then Dolfo approaches us and says, "Lita, my father and I have decided that it would be safer for Mely and Toti, our younger brother, to be in the province. They'll have many relatives there to protect them, the farm is well fortified, and the guerrilla movement is strong there. So, I will be taking them with me to Nueva Ecija tomorrow when I go back."

What a surprise. Mely and I look at each other, then she hugs me tightly, and with tears running down her cheeks, she says, "Lita I'll never forget you. I'll always think of you and our happy times together. And when this war is over, we will be back and we'll get together again."

I don't know what to say; I am angrier about the war than sad at the parting. So, I agree with her, "yes we will see and be together again after this war."

Then her mother calls her and says, "Mely we have to start your packing." And Mely turns away to follow her mother upstairs.

I go home, sit on the sofa and tell Mother about it and say, "that's another unhappiness that this war is causing."

Mother sits next to me and says, "yes. But let's be thankful we are alive, and for now safe, and not suffering real deprivation. Soon, we hope and pray, it will be over and we can go back to normalcy and true peace."

Waiting for Arrival of American Forces

Now that Mely is gone, my friendship with Chic (pronounced "cheek") M. develops a closeness. She is one of the nieces of Mr. Congressman. They are not next-door neighbors. They live at the corner of Cataluna and Espana in a big two-story house that occupies half of the block from Cataluna to Eloisa. A whole extended family lives there—the Congressman's mother and all his siblings and the respective families of the married ones. The Congressman, however, has his own home in another street off of Espana.

Chic and I have gotten acquainted during those fund-raising drives. We share a love of reading and so on those occasions we would tell each other stories we have read in school and discuss them. But because we don't live close to each other, we seldom get together. Now that school is out, she gets to watch and take care of the drugstore that her pharmacist uncle owns. It is on the first floor of their big house at the corner of Cataluna and Expana and opens out to those streets.

In another part of that first floor is a big room full of books on book shelves and bookcases. It is a kind of library and books range from textbooks to books on history, art, philosophy, economics, to novels, literary and modern romance and science fiction. So Chic invites me to keep her company in the drugstore as we read and talk about some of the books. It is very exciting and entertaining; we get to read and talk about *The Count of Monte Cristo*, *The Man in the Iron Mask*, *The Three Musketeers*, *Rebecca*, and others. When I go there, I take Tommy and Rey and they play with Chic's younger sisters about their own age.

In front of the drugstore, across Cataluna, is a *sari-sari* (a general store, usually the first floor of a house that ordinarily is the living room and eating area) like our neighborhood co-op; the difference is that this sells retail and more popular items for the children, like candies, fruits, toys, and comics.

One day, Tommy says, "*Ate*, can you buy me bubblegum at the *sari-sari* store?" I say, "sure."

Mother always gives me money whenever I go out, with or without my brothers; at the end of the day when I don't spend it I return it to her but she says. "Keep it and save it for another time when you might need to pay for something that costs more than what I give."

So, today we stop at the *sari-sari* store before going to see Chic at the drugstore. We make the acquaintance of the storekeeper, Andy (about fifteen years old), the youngest son of the owners who are active members of the neighborhood association. Tommy is a very sociable and friendly child, and before long he and Andy become good friends and he starts spending more time there than with us. I see them talking to each other across the display counters when there are no customers. Nobody, except those tending the stores, is allowed behind the counters. Same rule applies to the drugstore. When Andy is busy with customers, Tommy reads comics. Tommy is also learning practical arithmetic like giving the right change back.

Landing of American Troops on Leyte

After breakfast today, Mr. Villa drops in and excitedly tells Father: "Tom, according to my short-wave radio, General MacArthur made a successful landing on Leyte yesterday after a successful amphibious assault the day before. What's puzzling is that he met with little resistance from the Japanese."

Father says, "maybe because they did not expect him there and on that day. Remember, even Dolfo did not know where and when he was going to strike."

Mr. S. knocks and opens the door and says, "Dolfo has just arrived and is having breakfast. Why don't you come over and have lunch with us. I already called Mr. A. and asked him to call the others."

I tag along with Father and Mr. Villa because I want to see Dolfo and ask about Mely. When Dolfo sees me he comes over and gives me a big hug. He says, "That's from Mely. She says to tell you that she misses you and wishes she were here or that you were there."

"I know. I miss her too."

They sit in the combined living room and dining area. Mr. Villa tells them about the news of General MacArthur's successful landing on Leyte, Dolfo says, "Yes, the amphibious assault on Leyte Gulf began two days ago, October 23, (1944)."

I say, "isn't that Mely's birthday."

"Yes," Dolfo says. "That is why she was thinking of you and how you both would fight for the crunchiest *lechon* (roasted whole pig) skin."

Mr. Villa says, "I'm just wondering. The news says that they met with very little resistance."

"That's true. The Japanese were expecting the assault on either the big island of Mindanao to the South or the big island of Luzon to the North. Not the Visayan islands, and not Leyte. So they sent their forces to Luzon and Mindanao, leaving the Visayas practically defenseless. Moreover, the guerrillas in the area have been informed by the underground and they helped secure the island by making sure roads and bridges were not mined and keeping the Japanese busy with minor skirmishes."

Someone asks, "When do you think they will be reaching us?"

Dolfo says, "Hard to say because as they move northward, they have to secure all the other islands so that their backs are safe. One thing sure is that General MacArthur wants the speediest way to Manila to liberate the POW and the internees, and take over Malacanang Palace (the President's office and residence, seat of the government)."

Attacking the University of Santo Tomas Campus

The thoughts of liberation so close raise the hopes and relieve the tension. Christmas, 1944, seems cheerier; people hug each other and stop to chat after the Christmas morning mass. More people are smiling. The gatherings at the

Christmas meals are bigger as people pool what they have and share with relatives and neighbors.

This morning, a bit chilly, as we come out of the Santo Tomas church after the mass of the Feast of the Three Kings—January 6, 1945—Mr. Villas rushes toward Father and, with a lot of excitement, says, "Tom, today the United States navy entered the Lingayen Gulf and started to engage the Japanese navy defending the Gulf and begin the bombardment of the Lingayen beaches." Lingayen is a coastal city, the capital of the province of Pangasinan, north of Manila, a bit north of Corregidor.

I look at Father and at Mr. Villa, and I remember a similar scene, many years ago it seems. It was December 8, 1941, the Feast of the Immaculate Conception, and the message was sad: the U.S. Installation at Pearl Harbor was destroyed by the Japanese who were coming toward us to invade. I was nine then. Today, the tables have been turned, the tides have changed; it is the U.S. Armed Forces invading to liberate us. What a happy message. Father and Mr. Villa are smiling, yet I notice the lines of worry etched on their faces and their dark hair had turned almost gray from the years of hardship. They seem to have grown old prematurely. I will be thirteen in May.

Everybody has started to listen to the short-wave radio. After three days, January 9, Lingayen is made secure and the march toward Manila begins. In the first week of February, Dolfo comes home. He is accompanied by two young men, who like him, are wearing holstered revolvers and their sheathed hunting knives and their belts have slots for bullets. I've never seen Dolfo armed before; he looks older and more serious. He tells the neighborhood association group gathered at his parents' house,

> Today the U.S. Forces entered Manila and are making their fastest drive toward Malacanang Palace, the University of Santo Tomas, and the Bilibid Prison. They are guided and led by guerrillas who know the quickest and safest way. They will soon be at Santo Tomas. So, I'm asking all of you to lock and barricade your front doors and close your front windows. Do not go out, or even look out, whatever it is you might hear. The safest place is the middle of your houses. I also suggest that you cook and eat your supper early.

Since September with the first sighting of U.S. planes in the Philippine skies and the constant blaring of air-raid sirens, Father has decided to have us sleep downstairs. All our townhouses are identical; the walls all around the ground floor are concrete, about the height of an adult waist. The wooden staircase, against one side of the wall, descending toward the back of the house, ends in a concrete landing with two concrete steps turned toward the room. This is the same setup with our next-door neighbor; their staircase against the shared wall. So Father has decided that this is the safest place. He has placed the heavy dining table under the staircase and topped it with all our extra pillows and blankets. Under it we sleep on mats on the floor. Father also has placed the widest and heaviest bookcase at the end of the table, facing the front door, right behind the heavy sofa. Against the opposite wall, Father has moved the lighter wooden kitchen table from the outside and lined the two narrower bookcases at the end of it facing the front window; Father sleeps here, sometimes with Tommy. He has left his heavy office desk in the front room, the way it has always been because he has been seeing clients there.

Tatay Iboy and Tiyeng have been with us since mid-January knowing that Father would need help. The house of *Lolo* Anong (his brother-in-law) where they are staying is nowhere close to any possible target. Moreover, *Lolo* Anong has three grown teenage sons. *Tatay* Iboy sleeps under Father's desk protected by the front and side concrete walls. The mosquito nets are draped over the top of the tables.

We finish supper by 6:30, have the kitchen cleaned up, and all of us ready for bed. Tiyeng brings in two large earthen jugs of drinking water; *Ate* Nene brings in three chamber pots and a half a gasoline can of water; and Mother brings in two large thermos of freshly boiled water. The heavy black drapes are down and so we can have light. Father and *Tatay* Iboy have large flashlights and lots of batteries. Mother has her bag of medicines and medical supplies, and we, the children, except Rey, have our own backpack of clothing.

Tommy and Rey are asleep by 7:30; Mother, Tiyeng, and *Ate* Nene, sometime after 8:00. Father and *Tatay* Iboy are still talking to each other softly. At about 9:00, as I am getting under the blanket after finishing a *Sinbad the Sailor* adventure, we hear a crash coming from the direction of Santo Tomas followed by a barrage of gunshots. Then more crashes and more gunshots.

Father and *Tatay* Iboy both sit up and listen intently. Father says, "Those sound like tanks crashing and storming the walls. And probably exchanging fire with the Japanese."

Then silence for a long while. Suddenly there is a lot of running on the street and voices shouting and repeating, "the Americans have entered UST."

Father and *Tatay* Iboy continue to listen where they are. After a long while, everything is quiet and we decide to go to sleep.

Meeting Our Liberators

I wake up to the smell of breakfast cooking. Tiyeng begins serving it at the kitchen table under which Father sleeps. But Father is now under the heavy table and Mother is serving him hot cocoa while she piles blankets over him. Mother says, "He started malaria attack at about 4:00 this morning. I've been giving him hot tea to stop the chills."

We clean up after breakfast. All the sleeping mats, except the one Father is on, have been rolled and put away. The window is opened and the black drape pulled down. Then there's a knock on the door and Dolfo saying through the open window, "Successful assault on UST; the internees are safe. The Japanese surrendered and asked to be allowed to join their troops retreating to the south of Manila across the Pasig River. So, everybody come out and meet your liberators."

Ate Nene, Tommy, and I go out; *Tatay* Iboy and Tiyeng look out the window; and Mother and Father are seated on the sofa facing the open door. And we see American soldiers, walking single file on each side of our street, from Espana to Isabelo de los Reyes, their rifles across their torso with the muzzle pointed upward, and NO BAYONETS! The children closer to Espana are waving little American Flags with their left hand and the index and middle fingers of their right, extended in a V shape, gleefully shouting "Victory Joe, Victory Joe!"

I look at the Americans and see tall, slender men, with white skin like those of our nuns from Spain and the non-Filipino Jesuits. They have helmets on so I can't tell what color hair they have. Some of them salute Dolfo, who is standing next to me and who now wears an armband, and he salutes back. A soldier, not in a khaki uniform and without a gun, comes up to us and hands Tommy a little American Flag and three lollipops; he also gives me a flag and two bars of "Babe Ruth." And so Tommy and I start waving the flag and our V and saying "Victory Joe."

A big high truck with soldiers seated opposite each other passes by and Dolfo says, "That's a six-by-six used to transport troops. This one following (a lower but much wider truck, also with seats opposite each other) is a weapons carrier, and the two smaller open-sided vehicles behind it are jeeps."

Another guerrilla approaches Dolfo and whispers something. Dolfo nods his head and says, "Don't worry, I'll take care of it." And he goes toward Isabelo de los Reyes.

As I stand alone with Tommy, a vehicle, all closed up with a red cross on a white circle on its side, passes by then stops. A man next to the driver gets off and comes toward me, hugs me and says, "Isabelita, I am so glad to see that you are all right."

I haven't heard that nickname in a long time. I look at him and, happily, say, "Mr. E.! How is Mila and the rest of the family?" (Mila was one of my close friends at Santa Isabel College from grades 3 to 5, and Mr. E. drove the school bus.)

"We are all fine and safe, thank God. What about your family?"

"We are all all right and safe except for my father."

Mr. E. looks worried and asks, "Is he injured? What happened to him?"

"No, sir. He has malaria. He's been taking quinine and aspirin for fever."

"Quinine is good to relieve the symptoms. But it does not cure. There is a new medicine that is an effective cure. Take me to him." That's when I notice that he has a white armband with a red cross on it.

When I introduce him to my parents, he shakes Father's hand, then takes his pulse, and says, "You are on the fever stage. I have a new medicine that effectively cures malaria, not just relieves it. It is called "Atabrine." The American troops afflicted with malaria have been taking it and have been cured. Take it twice a day—at breakfast and at supper—during an attack, and once a day when not. It may turn your skin yellow, but that is just coloring, not a liver effect. Here are two bottles, good for three months." My parents thank him. He returns to the waiting bus.

Fleeing the Conflagration

One morning, Mr. Villa drops in and says, "The Americans are setting up a food distribution center on the UST campus in front of the church and they are inviting everyone to come and get food supplies. These are free. Bring a big shopping bag."

Tatay Iboy, Tiyeng, *Ate* Nene, Tommy, and I go to the UST grounds. Mother stays with Father who is still weak from the malaria attack. As we get near the campus, we hear lots of laughter and merriment. We see the cement wall on P. Noval street down in rubbles. As we enter we see many children running and playing on the grass, and many U.S. soldiers, none of them carrying rifles, standing by watching them or walking around to see that everything is in order. And more unarmed soldiers helping hand out the packets of food from 2 six-by-six trucks parked on the wide pavement in front of the church. And the people just walk up to the truck and are helped immediately. There are some soldiers who are armed, but they seem to stay out of sight.

And I remember a similar scene, many years ago, when we lined up to buy staples from a store set up by the Japanese, armed guards with bayonets walking up and down the line, and the fear of being pulled out, slapped or bayoneted for reasons only they could think of.

The packets of food contain generous supply of a big can of butter, two "American" bread (loaves, our bread is a crusty roll), cans of "chili con carne," corned beef hash, potted meat and deviled ham, small cans of Nescafe, cans of evaporated milk, a square can, with a round opening on top, of soda crackers. What a feast! All the things we have been deprived of. The children are given candies (Babe Ruth, O'Henry, Chuckles [my favorite], Chiclet, bubblegum), biscuits, and toys. When we thank the soldiers for the packets, they say, "Come back anytime and as often as you wish or need to." Such kind people!

The following day, Dolfo assembles the "elders" of Cataluna while his three friends, do the same for P. Noval, Eloisa, and Adelina. He says,

> We have just been informed that the Japanese who retreated to South Manila across the Pasig River have decided to fight back

> instead of surrendering. They blew up the three major bridges—Quezon, Sta. Cruz, and Jones—moved in and set up defensive positions in Intramuros (the walled city built by the Spanish government for their offices, schools, churches, and beautiful big Spanish-style homes). To retaliate against their loss, they will be shelling Santo Tomas and Bilibid Prison. The possibility of your neighborhood being hit is great. So I suggest that you start on getting ready to move away.

Without transportation, except Dr. M. who has a car, it is suggested that everyone build a pushcart. *Tatay* Iboy contacts Berto, his former chauffeur, and his brother to help him build ours. They use the patio to build one the size of a double bed and deep enough to push out of the door with the wheels on. We pack pillowcases with all the essentials, this time including the canned goods. Mother has her medicine bag and two thermoses of boiled water; Tiyeng packs the two earthen jars of drinking water, mats and mosquito nets. And we, the children, have our own backpack. *Tatay* Iboy and Father have made sure that the cart is not overloaded that they, Tiyeng included, cannot push or move it.

The cart stands upright by the door, ready to push out; all the packs are on the floor ready to be thrown into the cart in assigned places, once it is out. Mother and Rey will be seated in the center surrounded by all the packs. *Ate* Nene, Tommy, and I will be walking alongside the cart.

Early this morning, the bombardment of UST starts. Dolfo and his men are knocking on all the doors telling everybody to get out. Father, *Tatay* Iboy, and Tiyeng push out the cart to the wide sidewalk. Dolfo and two of his men help put it down from the sidewalk to the street, then he turns around to help me and *Ate* Nene load the packs. Mother climbs in with Rey and sits in the center facing backward, tightly surrounded by the packs. The cart starts moving; we are headed north to Bangbang Street, at the invitation of Dr. M., where their relatives have a big house that can accommodate us also.

The street begins to fill up with all kinds of pushcarts and people running. We have just passed our next-door neighbor's house when we hear the whine of a cannon shell. We drop to the ground as close to the sides of the cart;

Tommy and I between the front and back wheels and *Ate* Nene between the two front ones. Mother pushes Rey between two packs and bends down to a crouch and leans between a tall pack and a big pack. Tiyeng is behind us and Father and *Tatay* Iboy at the back. We hear the explosion behind us and see the house that is hit go up in flames.

Father says, "They are using incendiary bombs. That is dangerous because they don't care about targets or directions; they just want to start a conflagration."

So they speed up and Tommy, *Ate* Nene, and I start running to keep pace. Another whine and another, and more houses flare up. At one point, Mother gasps and sobs quietly; she has just seen our house hit and go up in flames. Father says repeatedly and soothingly, "It can all be replaced."

Suddenly, a sidewalk and a house ahead of us are hit and burst into flames. *Ate* Nene, who will be sixteen in July, runs to the back of the cart and helps push it to make it go faster. After we cross Isabelo de los Reyes, we slow down. It seems that the shelling is not going that far. Mr. Ar., the neighborhood association president of these blocks, invites us to rest a while and gives us some food; we have not had time to eat breakfast.

Living a Nomad's Life

The two-story house of Dr. M's relatives is very large. But it is crowded because there are some other fire-refugee relatives from the Bilibid Prison area. *Tatay* Iboy and Tiyeng return to *Lolo* Anong's place in Oroquieta, not far from Bangbang.

Today, two days after we arrive, Father goes out to contact his law partners and see if they know of houses or apartments for rent. He comes home with Judge L., a very good friend and the godfather of Rey, who invites us to his home in Don Quijote, two streets from Santo Tomas, on the other side, and behind my former school, the Instituto de Mujeres on Gov. Forbes. This area is not at all damaged or attacked. The shelling is stopped when the U.S. forces cross the Pasig River and are now battling the Japanese to liberate South Manila.

The house is big; we stay in one of the two front bedrooms on the second floor. They are very kind and accommodating and understanding. They and their three sons stay in the two back bedrooms. Mrs. L. loves music and asks me to play the piano every evening after supper.

Two days after we move in, the other front bedroom gets occupied by two U.S. army officers. They stay much to themselves; we hardly see them because they leave very early in the morning and come home at night at bedtime. They are nice and polite and greet us whenever we meet. From them we learn about the amphibian tanks crossing the Pasig River and the pontoon bridges built by the U.S. Army Corp of Engineers, that are placed on the surface of the water spanning the river and allowing trucks and troops to cross behind the tanks.

One day, a nephew of Mrs. L. comes to stay. He and his family lived in South Manila and he, the lone survivor in his family, was rescued by the liberating army. They let him stay in one of the back bedrooms. From him we learn of the rumored "massacre" of civilians by the Japanese who vented on them their anger, shame, and frustration at being defeated and asked to surrender. The American liberators have won; South Manila is secure, but the battle is not over yet. There are still so many places to liberate and secure. And the Japanese are not surrendering.

Today, we notice that the house is quiet; the children are not around. When Mother asks the niece about Mrs. L., she tells us that the whole family has moved to their large three-bedroom apartment in Ermita (South Manila), which survived destruction and is now vacant. Father decides it is time for us to move on; he has told the judge many times about it, but they have insisted on us staying on.

So Father goes back to Cataluna, a most familiar place to start from. He talks to Mr. Ar., again inquiring about places to rent. Mr. Ar. says,

> Tom, so far there are none I know of around here, and people are not thinking of rebuilding right now. Everything is still so unstable. What I can do is let you stay, temporarily, in the upper part of my automotive repair shop next to my residence. There is not much business and so my manager and his wife who lived there are in the province. Then that will give us time to look around.

And so we move back to Cataluna.

In church this first Sunday after our move back, we see a lot of people we know and so after mass there is a lot of hugging and chatting. Andy (Tommy's friend who tended their *sari-sari* store) and his family are there. They moved to the house of his older sister who also has a store, across Espana; this area, too, is not damaged. He invites Tommy to visit the store saying that he has a lot of new comics. So, Tommy, who has made a lot of new friends in our new area, goes on Saturdays to Andy's new store. He leaves after breakfast and returns at lunchtime.

Wondering How Many More Sufferings to Bear

At abut 9:00 AM today, Mr. F. of Adelina Street, one of Father's former neighborhood association leaders, rushes to Father and says,

> Tom, Tommy was hit by an American weapons carrier while he was crossing Espana and was thrown toward the grassy median. But apparently his head struck the cement curb; there's blood there. Before I and Andy, from the other side of Espana, and other people could get to him, someone from the weapons carrier got down, picked him up and drove away. We shouted at them to stop, but they just sped away.

Father says, "let's all start looking for him; check all hospitals, private and public, and clinics, nearby and far. Even churches, I'm going to the American base and file a report on it." Then he goes out with Mr. F. to join the search. Mother sits by the front window looking angry and frustrated because she couldn't join the search, but mostly worried because she does not know what Tommy's condition is.

Lunchtime and still no word about Tommy. None of us could eat. Mother keeps looking at the door hoping Tommy would just walk in as he usually does at about this time, saying, "I'm hungry."

At about 6:00 PM, a young man drops in and says, "Attorney, we just found Tommy. He is at the North General Hospital."

"That one at the end of Espana where it forks into two streets? That was the first one we inquired at and they said they knew nothing of a child hit by a motor vehicle. Of course their emergency room was packed."

Mother asks, "how is he?"

The young man says, "he looks all right; his head is bandaged. He just looks so lonely and sad. And he needs a clothes change."

Mother says, "I'm going to see and be with him right now," and she walks out the door.

Father turns to me and says, "Lita, go with your Mother."

I get a towel and a change of clothes for Tommy and run after Mother. She can never go through our street with all the debris—so much devastation, all the houses razed to the ground, we could not even recognize which was our house. So we go by way of P. Campa, two streets away.

Tommy is so happy to see us as we are happy to see him. Hugs and kisses. Mother asks for the doctor. He says,

> He has no concussion. It is a scalp wound. X-ray and EEG tests show everything is normal. He did not suffer any broken bones anywhere else. The Americans paid for everything that is needed—medication and medical supplies and procedures, and nutrition.

Mother asks, "when can he go home?"

"He could go home tomorrow evening. I'd like to observe him another day. Better yet, spend another night. I'm worried about the swelling and the headaches. He needs ice to control the swelling and we're almost out of it. The nurses have been freezing face towels with the ice, and these we use as supplements."

I say, "I know where I can get ice. I'll go right now."

Mother says, "Wait a minute! Where are you going?"

"Mother, remember the ice cream man who goes down our street peddling ice cream from a small pushcart every morning? He should have ice."

"But do you know where he lives or where he has his shop?"

"Not his house or shop exactly, but he once told us that he lives on Dapitan

Street and when I get there maybe his shop will have a sign at the door or any of the residents will know where he lives."

"Lita, that's four long blocks from here."

"That's all right. I'll run. Tommy needs the ice. I'll get the small pail from the house."

Mother says, "on your way back, please bring my nightgown and a towel. I will be staying here with Tommy for the night." Tommy looks up at Mother happily.

As I run home to get the pail, I am thinking that if there were no war, there would be no shortage of ice at the hospital, and if there was, *Tatay* Iboy could supply them from his ice-making factory in Manila that produced and sold blocks of ice where needed, and to keep the fish from their ponds fresh in their stall in the open market in Manila. The Japanese had taken them away and eventually destroyed them. Then, too, if there were no war, our houses would not have burned down and Tommy did not need to cross Espana to see Andy.

When I get home for the pail, *Ate* Nene is cooking supper. I tell them about Tommy's condition, what I'll be doing, and what I need to take back to the hospital.

Father says, "Why don't you stop a while and have something to eat."

Ate Nene says, "the fish is still frying, but the chicken soup is ready,"

I tell them, "I can't. Tommy needs the ice and right now they are substituting frozen face towels."

When I reach Dapitan, I see the store sign right away. Mr. Ice-cream man is surprised to see me but he and his wife let me in right away. I tell them everything and he says, "That pail of yours is so small; it won't hold much and half of it will be melted by the time you get to the hospital. Can you carry a gallon of ice? I'll have to put it in another metal container surround it with more ice so they won't melt fast."

"Yes, sir, if we make a backpack of it. Sir, I don't have money to pay for it. But when I return the containers tomorrow, I will work for you; help you make ice cream or clean up, and you don't have to pay me."

His wife hugs me and says, "My dear. You don't have to do that. We love to help children and see them happy. We wanted children but we were not blessed with any. That is why we are in this business; it gives us the opportunity to make children happy. Now show *Mang* ("mister") Juan about that backpack."

He looks at the two loops, like wings coming out of each side of the container at the top, and says, "I'll make it better."

He unties the loops and puts the ice containers into a small burlap sack and ties one end of each rope to the top and the other end to the bottom making a longer loop. Then he puts it on my back and says, "Now this is better. The container's bottom is also secure and will not be bouncing and hitting your back as you run. The burlap sack will protect your back from the cold."

His wife says, "I know you have not eaten yet going through all these. So here's something to munch on," and she puts two bananas and two oranges in my pail. I thank her, and silently thank God for kind and caring people.

When I get to the house, *Ate* Nene has Mother's nightgown and towel and another change for Tommy inside a pillowcase bound like a backpack. She also has included their toothbrushes, but not toothpaste; we only have one tube for everybody's use.

Father says, "that's all right. They can use salt, if the hospital cannot spare some."

Ate Nene says, "Tomorrow I'll go to the stores and see if they have any available. If not, I'll go to the American base and get what they can spare."

The Americans have been very kind in supplying the people with anything they need that is not available in the stores and which they can spare.

Ate Nene then takes off my backpack of ice and transfers it to her back and she gives me the backpack of clothing, and says as we go out, "I'll clean up and put things away when we get back. Lita still has to eat."

Searching for Decent School Clothes to Wear

Sometime after Tommy has been home for a while and fully recovered, Mother tells Father,

> Tom, we really should be moving to a place of our own, especially before the residents of this place return. And I want another area. This one has only heartbreak and pain for me; first Vic's death, then the house and everything we worked for

> burning down, and then Tommy's accident. There is talk that schools will open in June. I want us, by then, to be settled in our own place—apartment or house.

Manila is now fully liberated and is peaceful. With the help of the Americans, it is being rebuilt gradually, especially the three bridges blown up by the Japanese: Quezon, Sta, Cruz, and Jones, so that the two Manila (North and South) are connected again.

Father says, "well, it would make it easier to find a place in a wider area of search. I thought you wanted it here where everything is familiar and the church is so close and you already know a lot of people."

So Father talks to Mr. Ar. who says, "well, if that is the case I have this house on Lipa Street, close to Legarda and Bustillos, the Sampaloc market on Legarda, and the Sampaloc Church of Our Lady of Loreto on Bustillos, all walking distance. It is a real house over a former automotive garage and shop and not just a one-bedroom apartment like the one you're in now. It is older but in good condition; we'll get people to check the plumbing and electrical connections and get as much of the junk out from the shop. We used to live there until my brother who worked for me decided to take it over and I moved here. They have since moved to Malate (across the Pasig) to start the business there. So, stay there and see if you like it. Then you can either rent it or buy it. I never offered it to you before because I thought you preferred living in this vicinity."

So we move in by the end of April. Mother likes the house because it is spacious and has potential for improvement. She likes the place because a street away from us is Bustillos, a thriving business/commercial street that has variety of stores and shops, Chinese restaurants, two churches. The big Sampaloc market is on Legarda where Bustillos ends.

Moreover, schools are convenient: the Ateneo de Manila (the Jesuit School whose building in Intramuros has been completely destroyed) has opened a grade school at the Nazareth School on Guipit street, not too far from our street and Tommy will enroll there; Arellano High School reopens in Legarda and *Ate* Nene will be going there; and the nuns of Santa Isabel College (whose building in Intramuros was leveled and burned down during the liberation) will be using some of the rooms at the Convent of

San Miguel Church Parish as classrooms at the invitation of the the parish priest, and I will be going there. Both *Ate* Nene and I will repeat the second year because there was not enough school time, from June to September last year (1944), when the first American planes came to start Liberation, and all the schools closed.

This parish is located at the end of the Legarda Extension/Tanduay Street (the street in front of Sta. Rita College) and close to the foot of Ayala Bridge. This bridge is one of the bridges not destroyed by the Japanese because the area was liberated and secured right away, taking the Japanese by surprise; it is close to the Malacanang Palace, the Philippine. President's office and residence.

One big problem all over the city is the lack of clothes—especially school clothes. So far no fabric stores have opened; no fabrics are being manufactured. The problem must have been brought to the attention of the Americans because they immediately set up centers for relief clothing. Of course, most of the clothes are big and long. Mother asks someone about renting a sewing machine, and they, after getting our address, send a Singer brand to our house, to the delight of my Mother, complete with lots of threads and needles and a pair of scissors at no charge.

There are two styles we find unusual but like very much: the jumper and the culottes, especially when combined—culottes with straps. So Mother picks up a lot of those for *Ate* Nene and me. Now for these jumpers, blouses are needed. Mother notices a nice shiny silk-like creamy white material, and she asks for it, in fact, for several. The American soldier helping out in the distribution, asks, puzzled, "Ma'am, how big an area are you going to cover?"

Mother answers, "a torso, the body's upper part."

The soldier, wide-eyed, says, "Ma'am, do you know what this is? It's a parachute!"

And Mother answers without hesitation, "young man, I don't care what it is. It will make several beautiful blouses and a few special-occasion dresses."

And so when school starts this June, *Ate* Nene and I will have beautiful silky blouses, some decorated with tatted lace and some embroidered with different color threads, all hand sewn by Mother and Tiyeng.

Enjoying a Revived Liberated City

In July of this year, 1945, a month after schools start, General MacArthur announces that the Philippines is now completely liberated and that General Yamashita, the Supreme Commander of the Japanese military in the Philippines, is being tried for war crimes, especially atrocities toward the American prisoners of war and against the civilians and that he will be convicted and will be hanged.

Rebuilding Manila begins in earnest. South Manila is the political, commercial, cultural, and educational center, and so begins the rebuilding of City Hall. The Legislative and the Commerce buildings, the Post Office, the Metropolitan Theater, the University of the Philippines and the adjacent Philippine General Hospital and College of Medicine, Ateneo de Manila (High School and College), and other convent schools not totally damaged.

Intramuros, the center of fierce fighting and the massacre of civilians during the liberation is in total ruins and nothing is being done to rebuild it.

The nuns of Sta. Isabel College have been working hard ever since their flight from Intramuros to get a building of their own. Their hard work during this summer school break (April and May) has paid off and they have acquired the Sta. Rita Hall on Taft Avenue and Ayala Boulevard and are able to offer classes in the Grade School, High School, and Collegiate.

So, in June 1946, a few days after my fourteenth birthday, I start my third year classes at the new Sta. Isabel College building.

The quickest and easiest way to get there is by Ayala Bridge which ends at Ayala Boulevard onto Taft Avenue. However, Ayala Bridge is not a public transportation thoroughfare.

Sta. Isabel has a school bus—a U. S. Army weapons carrier donated to the school and converted to an open mini bus—but only for the grade school students. We have to get to school on our own. It is not at all difficult because there are so many public transportation—surplus Army jeeps given by the Americans to those who could use them. Mr. Ar., who has started his automotive business again, has four which he, like all the others, has converted to passenger "jeepneys."

These jeepneys are colorful with beautiful designs and patterns painted on the sides, and can carry ten or twelve passengers. The jeep's body behind the driver is lengthened, and two bench like seats are built to face each other across an aisle leading to an open doorway, and a running board comes down from this doorway as steps.

A friend and classmate, who lives two streets away from us, and I meet at my house, walk to Bustillos to catch a jeepney to take us to Quiapo, one of Manila's commercial center. We transfer to another jeepney that goes through Quezon Boulevard to Quezon Bridge to Taft Avenue.

Although this is an indirect and longer way, the trip is interesting. The open sides of the jeepney let us see so many things and happenings along the way. Quiapo is busy again—it used to be desolate—lots of people on the streets and street vendors calling out their products. There are stalls on the big plaza in front of the Church of the Black Nazarene; it used to be filled with beggars, crippled, blind, war damaged. . . . And we get caught in the energy of the hustle and bustle.

Sometimes when we are stopped waiting for the jeepney to fill, we witness scenarios. One time we see an American soldier in khaki uniform at a busy street corner selling watches that are lined along his arm, from shoulder to wrist. Lots of men gather around him, looking, haggling, or buying. Then another soldier comes, talks to him, takes his arm, and casually leads him away.

Another time we see an American sailor, in his white uniform, slouched on the sidewalk, his back to the wall of the building behind him, one leg extended, drunk and half asleep. People pass by him without disturbing him. Then a jeep stops in front of him and two soldiers get down. These are dressed differently. They have holstered guns on one side of their hips and a short club-like stick—like the ones our policemen carry—on the other side; their pant legs tucked into boots. They have helmets with the lettering "MP." They approach the sailor, gently lift him up and put him in the back seat of the jeep and they drive away.

It is amazing how kindly, quietly, and swiftly these incidents end.

One other very popular and profitable business is the picture taking of pedestrians with handheld cameras that Americans give away to civilians or sell cheaply. The pedestrians photogrpahed are approached and given a piece of paper with an address and are told to pick up their pictures the next day for a fee. This odd way of earning a living started in late 1944 when the handheld cameras began appearing in the hands of a few civilians after that first sight of American airplanes in the skies in September.

Cheering the Awarding of Philippine Independence

There have been talks of the Philippines getting its independence. One day we are told that the United States has finally agreed to award it. So, on July 4th of this year, 1946, we, the students, are asked to assemble at the Luneta Park, Manila's national park, at 12:00 noon to witness this occasion.

The park is crowded with students from all the high schools and colleges, their school banners and colors waving in front of them, and priests, nuns, and teachers accompanying them; employees of the public and private offices, banks, and hospitals. We of the Catholic colleges wear our uniforms.

And on a big temporary grandstand built in front of the Rizal Monument are the Philippine government dignitaries led by the Philippine President Manual A. Roxas and the Archbishop of Manila. The American dignitaries are lead by the U.S. Ambassador and General MacArthur. It is festive with bands playing all kinds of music. Then the speeches start.

I am not listening; I am looking around and see the devastation, the destruction, the debris, and I wonder if we are ready for independence. We have just survived a war—the country, depleted and poor. I think of the damaged homes, the shattered families, the broken people. . . . I think of young guerrillas and Philippine Scouts who fought for this moment and miss this moment to accept the honor for their sacrifice . . . And I bow my head in silence.

Then a loud cheer of *Mabuhay* from the crowd, and I look up. I see all the young eager faces, and I feel the strength of commitment in their raised arms . . . all survivors, all fighters in their own way. And I begin to believe we are ready for independence, for gathered here today is the hope and the future of the country.

The Philippine flag is raised as the American flag is lowered. I stand erect and attentive as everybody, loudly sings the Philippine National anthem, proud in the knowledge that henceforth we will stand as an independent nation among nations and no longer be only a Commonwealth of the United States, but the Republic of the Philippines.

And the joyous resounding cheer rises and reverberates throughout the whole country:

MABUHAY ANG PILIPINAS, MABUHAY!

(LONG LIVE THE PHILIPPINES, LONG LIVE)!

In Memoriam

Father	Attorney Tomas M. Yumol, Sr.
Mother	Exaltacion Buenviaje Yumol
Tatay Iboy	Eusebio Buenviaje (Maternal grandfather)
Tiyeng	Rosario Buenviaje (aunt, Mother's older sister)
Ate Nene	Zoraida Buenviaje Bautista (aunt, Mother's younger sister)
Tommy	Attorney Tomas B. Yumol, Jr. (brother)

All the Philippine Scouts and American soldiers who died in the battlefields of Bataan and in the Bataan Death March, defending the Philippines and protecting its people.

All the Filipino guerrillas who in their own way contained the Japanese and minimized atrocities against the civilians and who guided and led the American Liberation Forces through the safest and swiftest way toward their goals.

All the American fighters who survived Bataan and Corregidor but decided to return with the Liberation Forces to win back for the Philippines and its people the right to Life, Liberty, and Happiness and enjoy freedom from fear and want.

God Bless Them All!

Index

All page numbers in italic indicate an image or map.

CPSIA information can be obtained
at www.ICGtesting.com
Printed in the USA
LVOW12s0906020616
490684LV00005B/10/P

9 781933 337685